ULL ITEM BARCODE

19 0714063 8

D0198659

EXPLORING THE UNCONSCIOUS

By the same author:

The End of War or the End of Mankind
  (Globe Publications, 1955)

The Failure of the Sexual Revolution
  (Kahn & Averill, 1974)

The Social History of the Unconscious
  (Open Gate Press, 1989)
  Paperback edition in two volumes:
Vol 1: Archaeology of the Mind
Vol 2: Civilisation - Utopia and Tragedy
  (Open Gate Press, 1992)

The Unknown Self
  (Open Gate Press, 1990)

EXPLORING THE UNCONSCIOUS

new pathways in depth analysis

GEORGE FRANKL

OPEN GATE PRESS
LONDON

SHL WITHDRAWN

BIBL. LONDON UNIV.

First published in 1994 by Open Gate Press
51 Achilles Road, London NW6 1DZ

Copyright © 1994 by George Frankl

All rights reserved

British Library Cataloguing-In-Publication Programme
A catalogue record for this book is available from the British Library

ISBN 1-871871-06-9

Printed in Great Britain by
Halstan & Co. Ltd., Amersham, Bucks

Contents

CONTENTS

Introduction

While Freud's explorations into the unconscious have had a profound impact upon modern literature and art and have influenced popular thought and language, we witness an increasing resistance towards his work among those who should be the main beneficiaries of his investigations, namely, the specialists in the human sciences. In sociology, psychology and psychiatry we find a renewed determination to ignore or belittle the contribution of psychoanalysis. It has become fashionable among the experts in human relationships and the treatment of psychological disorders to adopt a dismissive attitude towards the unconscious, practically an obligation amongst those who consider themselves to be scientific to proclaim that the hypothesis of an unconscious mind does not stand up to serious examination and has no empirical evidence to sustain it.

The resistance to psychoanalysis and the reluctance to accept or even acknowledge the unconscious probably has three main reasons: 1) The prevailing concept of 'the scientific', which upholds the view that any investigation which merits the name of science must be directed to facts of the objective world. Research which cannot be considered to be objective and capable of being tested empirically is at best regarded as non-scientific or, at worst, as non-sense (to use Wittgenstein's phrase). This view constrains psychology to a study of manifest behaviour, and directs psychiatry to the investigation of neurochemical processes. It tends to consider the mind and mental determinants of behaviour as being outside the scope of scientific study and therefore irrelevant. In viewing the individual as an object which can be properly investigated in his physical, biological, neurological and chemical aspects, they inevitably tend to minimise the importance of his subjectivity, of his subjective-mental experiences. 2) Psychiatry, psychology and the social sciences have become part of a bureaucratic system which deals with people as objects, to be treated, manipulated and engineered in the most efficient way possible, with the overriding aim of getting them back to normal life and to play a useful role in society. The bureaucratic system has no time nor any interest in an individual's internal, subjective processes. 3) The intellectual stagnation of psychoanalysis, its difficulties in facing the problems of modern mass society, its cumbersome, time-consuming, inefficient and statistically unpredictable method of treatment. Psychoanalysts seem unable to conduct experimental research to validate their theories or to improve the efficiency of their treatment methods.

One cannot avoid the impression that psychoanalysts have become intimidated by the hiatus of not being properly scientific and of having fallen behind in the competition for therapeutic efficiency; they have lost the intellectual confidence of being in the vanguard of psychological and psychiatric studies.

It is, however, high time to question the widely-held assumption that the scientific method, which has proven to be the supreme tool for the understanding and mastery of nature, can and must also be applied to the study of man's mind and his behaviour. On closer examination we come across some philosophical problems which make it questionable whether psychology – literally, a science of the mind – is at all possible. If we consider that science by its very nature deals with objects, phenomena occurring in the world outside the subject, then we must ask how it can deal with the occurrences within the subject. As mental processes – by which we mean a person's thoughts, feelings, desires, fears, fantasies and dreams – are subjective experiences, we have to concede that they cannot be approached as if they were objective phenomena residing in the world outside. To put it differently: the concept of scientific objectivity rests on the assumption that objects have an existence that is both external to and independent of the observer; they have the characteristics of spatial extension and mass, and the characteristics of time and causality. These characteristics of objects are designated as quantitative and are shared by all physical objects; therefore, the scientist, as a scientist, must make himself 'objective', he must exclude subjective considerations from his scientific work. The attempt to apply this concept of scientific objectivity to the study of the human mind must therefore be considered inappropriate.

The problem, reduced to its bare essentials, can be put in the following way: how can the subjective be the object of scientific research? This represents a 'philosophical knot' which has puzzled philosophers and scientists through the ages. The problem that confronts all possible psychology has been beautifully presented by Schopenhauer: 'That which knows everything which is known and is not known by anyone is the subject. It is thus the foundation and agent of the known world, the inevitable and constant condition for all appearances, all objects, for it is only for the subject that something exists. A subject is ourself insofar as we are the agents of knowledge and not the objects of knowledge. But even one's body is an object of knowledge, which we, therefore, from the point of view of the theory of knowledge, must consider as an object'. The body is object amongst objects and therefore dependent on the modalities which govern our perception and knowledge of objects. Like all objects, even our own body is manifest in space and time, dependent upon the categories of extension, substance and causality. The subjective mind, however, which thinks and feels is not part of these modalities. If, however, all that is known must appear as an object to the

3

thinking and knowing subject, and, more particularly, if science is constrained to the study of the objective world, how can the subjective be the object of scientific investigation?

Empirical psychologists and psychiatrists attempt to solve this problem by viewing people as objects to be studied and investigated as physical entities, namely their manifest behaviour and the functions of their nervous system. But they pay the price of admission to the natural sciences by a tacit agreement to ignore both subjectivity and mind; what goes on inside the subject, that which cannot be known objectively is excluded from their field of investigation. Behavioural psychologists, for instance, make detailed and experimental studies of the correlation between stimulus and reflex in order to explain the behaviour of animals and man, and consider that which stands between the stimulus and the reflex as a hypothetical entity of which little is known and presumably of which little needs to be known. Psychiatrists treat people as biological organisms and focus their attention upon neurophysiological and chemical processes, assuming that any behavioural or mental disturbance must have an organic cause. In the pursuit of what they consider to be the correct scientific method, they pay scant attention to the subjective-mental processes and fail to see them as valid data for investigation. In consequence, they remain largely unaware of the fact that there is a two-way link between psyche and soma – a causative interaction from mind to body as well as from body to mind – and that psychological disturbances can cause a wide range of organic disturbances. Mental processes can influence and determine organic functions and organic functions can influence the mind. This symbiotic interrelationship seems to escape their comprehension.

It is a paradox that with the enormous advances in our scientific capabilities some basic truths are in danger of being lost, much to the detriment of our understanding of man. There is no escaping the fact that in order to understand what goes on inside the subjective mind, a man's experience of his emotions, thoughts, fantasies, desires and fears, which have a powerful impact not only on his bodily functions but also on his perception of the world and his relationship to his environment, has to be studied in its own right, and considered as valid data for systematic and scientific investigation. There is no doubt that the meticulous investigations carried out by behaviourists into the reflexes of animals and men are highly interesting and valuable and that the progress of psychiatry in its various branches has enormously advanced our understanding of the nervous system. However, without an equally thorough investigation into our mental processes, empirical investigations will not contribute very much to our understanding of the human psyche, and the dogmatic belief that it does so will prove an illusion.

A human being, as Spinoza has pointed out, is both mind and body, subject and object, and cannot truthfully be reduced to being one or the other. In *An Outline of Psychoanalysis,* Freud's last work written shortly before his death, Freud provided what seems to me a simple and straightforward solution to the old mind/body problem: 'We know two kinds of things about what we call our psyche (or mental life): firstly, its bodily organ and scene of action, the brain (or nervous system), and, on the other hand, our acts of consciousness, which are immediate data and cannot be further explained by any sort of description.' In his own investigations Freud combined the two dimensions of mind – its physical as well as its psychical manifestations – bridging the major traditions of European thought and coordinating them into a unified concept. In doing so he managed to overcome the apparent opposites which have split European thinking into two opposite camps: the introspective tradition of the humanists and the empirical tradition followed by Dalton, Wundt, Helmholtz, Pavlov and many others.

Freud has made it possible for the most subjective and private of all human experiences to become a field for scientific investigations. This can be considered the most outstanding of all Freud's achievements, it can be called the Freudian revolution in science. It would be wrong to assume that he neglected the influence of external conditions upon the psyche; he constantly stressed the reality principle but at the same time investigated the influence of psychological factors upon our perception of reality. The interconnection between the subjective and the objective, the physical and the mental, presented for him possibly the most fascinating aspect of psychological investigations.

There can indeed be little doubt that the mental and physical dimensions of the psyche are parts of a whole which we perceive according to the point of view from which we look at it. The view of the observer will be determined by his training, his personality and his cultural background. One must also not forget a person's psychological disposition in his choice of viewpoint, and whether he is inclined to view the psyche as a physical apparatus or as subjective mental process. The various approaches have contributed to our knowledge, and we know a few things about the way in which the nervous system, its chemistry and in particular the brain can produce certain states of mind, and about the way the mind can influence the body and produce chemical organic changes and determine the pattern of a person's behaviour.

However, in the race for greater efficiency in the treatment of mental disorders the victory at this stage belongs to the physical party. The developments in biochemistry and neurology and in particular the startling advances in pharmacology have enabled psychiatrists to adopt what appears to be a fairly efficient and practical method of therapy. The pharmacological industry provides them with drugs for almost every known psychiatric disorder. Modern societies, which have a declared obligation to provide treatment for the masses of people who suffer from medical and psychiatric ailments, naturally favour a treatment method which is reasonably efficient, cost-effective and reliable and able to provide statistical evidence for its success rate. It has the advantage (or disadvantage, according to the way you look at it) of seeing people in the mass, the individual as a statistical unit.

The modern psychiatrist's workplace is the hospital, the laboratory and pharmacological institutions; he spends much of his time experimenting with drugs, and he sees patients as objects upon whom pharmacological products are tried out. It is, of course, acknowledged that people have minds, thoughts, anxieties, delusions and obsessions, but these are seen as information required for a proper definition of a syndrome for which classified drugs are available. This fits neatly into the state of mind of scientific technology with its expectation to solve any kind of problem as long as it can be reduced to physical causes. The time-consuming and unpredictable investigations into the hidden recesses of our minds and the psychoanalysts' obsessions with the unconscious are considered scientifically unsound and, from a socio-political point of view, old-fashioned and wasteful. They may have satisfied the life-style of the high bourgeoisie of the nineteenth and early twentieth century but are now seen as an indulgence, which modern society, with its health service and social security systems which have to cater for all classes, simply cannot afford. It has been said in criticism of psychoanalysis that it could offer too little to too few. Today this view is held more widely than ever.

However, the much vaunted efficiency of modern psychiatric practice, with its reliance upon drug therapy, ECT and surgical intervention into the brain, has increasingly come under question. Contrary to the optimistic claims put forward by the psychiatric establishment and the pharmaceutical industry, a growing number of patients and former patients are making their criticisms and complaints heard. Indeed, there is a growing body of discontent, a feeling of unease about the methods employed by modern psychiatry. While ECT reduces states of acute panic-anxiety and is useful as a treatment for paranoia, it induces an agonising experience of mental debility, acute feelings of numbness, disorientation and loss of memory apart from the shock and pain of the treatment itself.

Drug therapy is known to produce a great variety of side-effects, some more alarming than the original symptom, and patients frequently have to take drugs to counter the side-effects of the original drug. There is a widespread complaint that patients are forced by doctors and psychiatrists to submit to drug treatment for life without having the side-effects explained to them or, indeed, of being frequently misinformed about the consequences of the treatment. Even the officially available statistics show the inefficiency of psychiatric treatment methods. Of 190,000 patients admitted every year into hospitals and clinics the majority are released after four weeks, but the readmission rate has risen alarmingly. The cures, therefore, are short-lived and treatment has to be repeated in most cases. Besides this high rate of readmission in short treatment cases, some 32,000 patients have to remain in hospital for more than one year.

The impersonal attitude of most psychiatrists produces moreover a considerable narcissistic injury in patients during their various interviews. They complain that psychiatrists barely listen to their emotional disturbances and their stories; they feel denigrated as persons and resent what they consider to be patronising attitudes which make them feel they are being treated like children or idiots. This depersonalised attitude among many psychiatrists, who seem only to be interested in the scientific facts of a case, looking for genetic or neurochemical causes, reinforces in many patients that feeling of rejection and indifference from which they suffer in any case; it increases their self-doubt and ego weakness which play a significant role in their psychological breakdown.

One can give many examples of the shortcomings and disappointments of current psychiatric methods, but this gives no cause for complacency among psychoanalysts – their record is no better if examined critically. The disappointments with psychoanalytic treatment have been a source of concern to patients as well as therapists for many years now, while the failures of modern psychiatry have only recently become widely known. Despite its many achievements both in terms of therapy as well as theory, it is true to say that psychoanalysis has not lived up to its early expectations. Its inability to provide reliable data for improvement rates, its lack of scientifically verifiable methods of investigation and its inadequate definitions of cure are compounded by its considerable social short-comings. Its time-consuming and expensive therapeutic method puts it beyond the reach of the majority of people who suffer from psychiatric disturbances. There is some justification in the accusation that psychoanalysis by catering only for the well-to-do displays a degree of social irresponsibility. Those who speak for the ordinary people, the working class, have for many years accused psycho-analysis of being elitist, of being stuck in the bourgeois world from which it has sprung and incapable of meeting the needs of modern society.

There is another aspect of psychoanalytic practice which has come under heavy criticism, first expressed by Wilhelm Reich: that, with free association as the king-pin of analytical therapy, it relies almost entirely upon verbal association. This came naturally to the Viennese bour-geoisie, from whom Freud and his early followers drew most of their patients, with their capacity to articulate a wide range of emotions and experiences. No matter how revolutionary psychoanalytic theories may be, intellectually they are demanding, relying on a culture where articulation was highly esteemed and enjoyed, qualities which are now greatly diminishing amongst the majority of the population.

The problem of verbal association, moreover, relates not only to a conflict of cultures but to a more fundamental deficiency in psychoanalytic techniques. Its reliance upon free association and interpretation severely limits its ability to deal with the early periods in the life of an individual which precede verbalisation; it can only bring out unconscious processes as far back as verbalisation of ideas occurred and word-images were formed. It cannot, therefore, penetrate to the deep layers of the psyche which go back to periods before the second year in the life of an individual. These are contentious arguments, but it remains true that the preverbal, emotional expressions of the infant contain some of the most important elements of the unconscious mind, and any analyst can vouch for the difficulties of reaching this area by means of free association. Reich, who was perhaps the most insistent critic of the orthodox method, has pointed out that we can only read the unconscious if we understand 'emotional expression'. He claimed that whereas Freud opened up the world of unconscious thoughts, it was he, Reich, who succeeded in understanding emotional expressions through his method of character analysis and vegetotherapy. His method promised not only to succeed in penetrating to the deeper levels of the psyche, which are responsible for the majority of neurotic as well as psychotic disturbances, but also promised to be closer to the mentality of most contemporary patients, particularly the young. The spontaneous impulsive or infantile expression of repressed emotions is much more congenial to modern patients and more readily gains their cooperation than the rules of psychoanalytic treatment.

A great number of therapeutic systems have appeared in the last few decades, each promising to provide an effective and rapid cure for all kinds of ailments. We can trace two main therapeutic movements which branched off from the psychoanalytic stem, in some cases entirely taking their leave from it. On the one hand, there are those who take their cue from Reich's concentration upon the release of previously repressed emotional impulses of an essentially aggressive or sexual nature: encounter groups, marathon week-end catharsis, sensitivity training, touching courses and feeling games, primal screaming, aggressiveness raising, 'Reichian massage', EST and many others. Most of these practices, while pretending to be hostile to psychoanalysis, consist of taking one or two pieces of psychoanalytic and Reichian discoveries, procedures and insights, and transforming them into an entire therapeutic regime. They can be seen as oversimplifications or, indeed, deformations of the complex theories of Freud and Reich and their concepts of personality development, repression, character armour, pleasure anxiety and orgastic disturbance. On the other side, we find the psychoanalytic deviationists who, while claiming to adhere to the most important Freudian concepts, give prominence to the ego functions and to the patient's personality.

Encouragement of choice, freedom of the will and of the authenticity of the person is the king-pin of their therapeutic concepts. Among the initiators of this movement the most important are H S Sullivan, Heinz Hartmann, Erich Fromm, Karen Horney and Carl Rogers. Anna Freud too is often seen as an important contributor to this movement, which goes by various names such as ego psychology, interpersonal relationship theory, transactional psychology, counselling therapy and object relations theory. But in their attempts to encourage the development of the patient's personality and his ego functions, his freedom of choice and his responsibility in society, in order to provide a more realistic and practical method of treatment, they pay the price of having to divert attention away from the unconscious. While there is no doubt in my mind that the strengthening of the ego and the patient's expression of his whole personality are not only laudable but also therapeutically valid aims, we must never forget or ignore the unconscious and infantile sexuality, as Freud repeatedly tried to impress upon Jung when he still had some hopes for him.

The Neo-Freudian 'humanists', despite all their efforts to modernise psychoanalysis, have failed to advance our understanding of the deep layers of the psyche, and it is this which in my opinion continues to be the main task of psychoanalysis. By tending to neglect the role of the unconscious and of infantile sexuality in the aetiology of neuroses, they have – instead of bringing psychoanalysis up to date – unwittingly helped to undermine its credibility. By diverting attention from the unconscious determinants of a person's self-image and his relationship towards his fellow men, they undermine the significance of psycho-analytical contributions to our understanding of the human psyche. They have made it easier for the sceptics to dismiss the very foundations of psychoanalytic theory, when even psychoanalysts themselves talk of Freud as the pioneer whose work has led on to the presumably much more profound theories of the human mind developed since his time. In an almost condescending manner, Harry Guntrip writes that quoting Freud in psychoanalysis is beginning at last to be like quoting Newton in physics. Many critics, once again, uphold the supreme wisdom of commonsense, and we find some asserting sarcastically that they have never seen any manifestation of sexuality in their little children or that the concept of the unconscious is nothing but a literary metaphor. The old resistances against an acceptance of psychic processes (which are subject to repression) are as powerful today as they have ever been. But curiously enough, it is the intellectuals – specialists to a man – who provide the contemporary vanguard of the movement of resistance in the name of commonsense, realism, scientific empiricism or hard-nosed, no nonsense psychology.

We have to admit, however, that the chief reason for the retreat from a science of the unconscious is the sheer difficulty of its investigation. There is no doubt that the human psyche is by far the most complex of all natural phenomena and presents the researcher with problems which sometimes appear insurmountable. The unconscious possibly presents the human intellect with its most profound challenge: 'Know thyself' – to become conscious of those hidden areas of the mind which we all experience and which have the most profound influence upon our thoughts and actions, that elusive something which stubbornly and with extraordinary cunning resists our attempts to make it conscious and reveal its secrets to our understanding. Many researchers, who have made it their chosen field of study, have become discouraged and have retracted their curiosity from that unyielding entity to focus their minds upon more tangible and responsive areas of the psyche or, preferably, on external conditions which are easier to analyse. Every investigator knows how the unconscious areas of the mind after they seem to yield something to our gaze unfailingly draw curtain after curtain to retreat again to their secret lair! It is understandable under such conditions that having received some impressions – a few glimpses of the hidden world of our minds – we assume that it has been reclaimed for consciousness and brought back to the safe territory of commonsense and reason. It is often hard to admit that we have only encountered some shadow and that it has once more retreated from our grasp.

We may say that the unconscious is analogous to Kant's 'Ding an sich', the eternal noumenon of which we can only make conjectures, inspired guesses maybe but guesses nevertheless. Freud in many respects acknowledged this and he at least was aware that it is only through inter-pretations and reasonable inference that we can get some access to it. But I have never felt inclined to acquiesce to this limitation, for the analogy with Kant's 'Ding an sich', while apt in many ways, is not entirely correct. The unconscious represents not so much a world which is independent of the modalities of our perceptions but presents a great variety of drives, experiences and images which are stored in our minds and continue to influence the way we react to current experiences. Thus while we can ascribe to the unconscious the functions of the 'a priori' which condition our modes of perception and reaction, it is not something that is independent of and inaccessible to our understanding. It is true that our understanding of it is profoundly impeded by our repressions and defences, which have imposed severe limitations upon psychoanalytical research. The goal of encountering the unconscious not by interpretation and inference but by direct experience has prompted me to seek for an improvement in the techniques by which the defences, directed by the ego, could be overcome. As these defences are often incredibly complex and cunning, one has to construct a technique which matches their cunning and can respond to their complexities. The classical psychoanalytic techniques are, in my opinion, too simplistic and even naive, and are no match for the complicated strategies, adopted by the defence mechanisms, which keep the unconscious hidden.

The search for improved techniques therefore must be the goal of the serious researcher, and I have pursued it not only for the improvement and greater effectiveness of therapy but also in order to rehabilitate and expand the findings of psychoanalysis. It is my aim in this book to give an exposition of some of the techniques which I have developed in my psychoanalytic laboratory, namely the consulting room, and the insights which I as well as my patients have gained from them.

1 From Hypnotism to Psychoanalysis

1. ORIGINS OF PSYCHOTHERAPY

There can be no doubt that the most consistent and thoroughgoing method for the investigation of the unconscious areas of the human mind is provided by psychoanalysis. While Freud did not claim to have discovered the unconscious, and gave priority to poets and philosophers before him, he did claim to have discovered the scientific method by which the unconscious can be studied. In what was probably his last essay before he died in London in 1939, he wrote: 'The concept of the unconscious has long been knocking at the gate of psychology and asking to be let in. Philosophy and literature have often toyed with it, but science could find no use for it. Psychoanalysis has seized upon the concept, has taken it seriously and has given it a fresh content. By its researches it has led to a knowledge of characteristics of the unconscious mental which have hitherto been unsuspected, and it has discovered some of the laws which govern them. But none of this implies that the quality of being conscious has lost its importance for us. It remains the one light which illuminates our path and leads us through the darkness of mental life. In consequence, the special character of our discoveries, our scientific work in psychology will consist in translating unconscious processes into conscious ones, and thus fill in the gaps in conscious perception.'

Freud has thrown light upon a continent of the psyche that was previously in darkness; he has given names to psychic processes that were unknown and nameless before him, and extended our intellectual horizon and our language. However, in order to gain a proper understanding of psychoanalysis it is important to know how its theory developed in Freud's mind and the decisive influence of hypnotic phenomena for his discovery of the unconscious. An understanding of hypnosis is of particular interest to us in this book, as I have developed a way of incorporating it into psychoanalytic therapy – after it had been abandoned by Freud and neglected by his followers.

Freud repeatedly stressed that 'it is not easy to overestimate the importance of the part played by hypnotism in the history of the origin of psychoanalysis. From a theoretical as well as a therapeutic point of view, psychoanalysis has at its command a legacy which it has inherited from hypnotism.'

Since earliest times hypnosis has played an important, albeit unacknowledged role, not only as an instrument for healing diseases but also in religious rituals. One should also not underestimate its impact upon the development of cultures by means of mass suggestion, and its ability to produce a degree of mass hysteria and nationalistic, religious and ideological passions. And even in our time we have all too often witnessed how otherwise intelligent and decent people can be compelled to pursue barbaric and irrational goals under the influence of hypnotic powers possessed by fanatical rulers. Repetitive incantation of words and slogans, whose meanings are deliberately kept obscure, giving the impression of mystical significance, obsessive dance-like movements and a waving of arms and a stamping of feet and monotonous beat music have the effect of weakening the ego functions, frequently producing the collective trance and hallucinatory experiences which can be used to arouse unquestioned submission to a religious or political authority. There is in us a fateful attraction for being released from the confines or demands of reality, to a regression to primitive, infantile states of mind, particularly if they are shared by the community. Shamans and priests, as well as kings and rulers have been trained to induce in themselves and in their worshippers a state of trance by means of what we now call autohypnotic exercises. Their apparent ability to transcend the limitations of reality gives them an aura of omnipotence in their communities which enables them to acquire positions of dominance. Ritual incantation, not only in religious ceremonies but also in political rallies, induces people to identify with the superhuman powers of a tribal spirit or deity transmitted by the shaman, priest or ruler, and they feel that they acquire his strength and liberation from the limitations of their normal selves. Their rational functions are exchanged for an illusion of collective power. We find here a regression to a normally forgotten state of mind which prevailed during man's early history and was probably instrumental for his survival against overwhelming odds. The fears which would overwhelm an individual in the face of danger are forgotten in the upsurge of a collective passion, which would enable him to confront his adversaries, to endure hardships and perform great feats of courage. In our time, Nuremberg rallies and Stalinist mass meetings come to mind, and also more recently the Holy Wars, when young men are ready to sacrifice their lives for causes which promise the glory of conquest and a privileged position in heaven as martyrs. We see here the ambiguity of selfless sacrifice to an ideal as well as the reactivation of unconscious passions of aggression and sadism. The passions induced by the hypnotic powers of rulers and priests can serve the highest aspirations as well as the most destructive and primitive drives of men.

Religious, racial, nationalistic fanaticism has always played a profound role in cultures and has shaped societies. An understanding of the hypnotic process involved may help us to resist these manifestations of regression to the archaic and infantile, and at the same time a study of such cultural and social processes can also teach us a lot about hypnotism. As in this book we shall be dealing with the therapy of individuals, I shall say a few words about the way hypnosis developed from its magic and mystical forms to a more scientific method and became a seminal influence in the origins of psychoanalysis.

It is well known that the priests of Ancient Egypt had cultivated hypnotism in their religious rituals and were highly skilled in using it for healing diseases. Among the ancient Israelites hypnosis was used by the rabbis of the northern or Galilean school of medicine, which practised what we would call nowadays a psychosomatically-orientated healing method, while the southern school was more medically orientated. It is very probable that Jesus was a Galilean rabbi and as such well-versed in hypnotism, which he used with striking success as a healer. His cures must have appeared miraculous to many of his contemporaries, so that they considered him inspired or possessed by divine powers. Indeed, the scriptures explicitly declare that it was his performance of miracles which proved his divinity.

However, we can no longer be content to explain the often quite astonishing physiological as well as mental changes which can be achieved through hypnotism, by reference to supernatural powers. It might be said that we have all been indoctrinated by Hume's declaration that 'any statement or claim which does not contain abstract reasoning concerning quantity or number, or any experimental reasoning concerning matters of fact and existence, should be committed to the flames; for it can contain nothing but sophistry and illusion.' We demand scientific explanations for so-called miraculous cures. But once we do so, our attention is drawn to previously unrecognised powers of the mind not only to cure psychosomatic, psychotic and neurotic diseases but also to cause them. If the mind under the influence of hypnosis can produce muscular paralysis, changes in metabolism, disturbances in the respiratory as well as circulatory functions and produce hallucinations and fantasies which are similar to those which occur in psychotic individuals, a new field of psychological and medical investigations appears before us.

2. FROM MAGIC TO SCIENCE

It is no coincidence that the first determined attempts to find an empirical explanation for hypnosis took place during the eighteenth century, when medicine set itself the task of emancipation from the religious world-view and to construct a science of medicine on empirical grounds. Hypnotic phenomena had to find an explanation in terms which seemed acceptable to science, independent of any religious, magical or miraculous interventions.

Mesmer, generally considered the father of psycho-therapy, found a way of explaining hypnosis in the treatment of his patients by relating its curative processes to a magnetic force which he called animal magnetism. He claimed that this force operated in all nature, and the healer only had to find a way of channelling it to the patient by a certain technique. Many physicians of Mesmer's time, following the teachings of Galen, believed that there is an invisible fluid or energy that pervades the universe, enriches the earth and all living organisms. If this energy enters living organisms, including humans, then good mental and physical health is maintained. If, however, this energy is blocked from entering the organism then an imbalance and disturbance takes place. It is necessary, therefore, to maintain a balance between the organism's need and external conditions in order to ensure good health, both mental and physical.

Another idea, which had existed since Paracelsus, was that the stars influence human beings through magnetism, and that magnets have an effect upon humans. With their powers of polar attraction and repulsion they have the power to harness the cosmic or ethereal energy. Van Helmont took this idea a step further and proposed that each person radiated 'animal magnetism', which would influence the mind and body of others. The practice of laying on of hands, mostly used by faith-healers, once again tends to revert to the idea that the cures they bring about are due to divine powers rather than animal magnetism.

In his doctoral thesis, Mesmer (1734-1815) dealt with the possibility that the stars and planets exercise a healing power, and that to be healthy an individual must be in electrochemical equilibrium with the planets. If this equilibrium is disturbed ill health will result, but equilibrium and, therefore, good health can be restored by means of magnets. With the help of Father Hell, a professor of astronomy at Vienna University, Mesmer designed an assortment of magnetised plates which he placed on affected or diseased parts of his patient's body, so that they would attract the cosmic energy required for healing. Later Mesmer concluded that he himself was a magnet, a repository and transmitter of the life force, and that by his touch and stroking he would guide the healing fluid through the human body to enter the 'substance of the nerves' of his patients and affect them immediately. In this way he thought he could provide a scientific explanation for his cures which would otherwise have been considered miraculous.

It is, however, interesting to note that it was precisely his claim to deal with natural processes, rather than relying upon miracles or divine intervention, that brought the wrath of the medical establishment upon his head. He was driven out of Vienna, and then, after he had formed a very successful practice in Paris, was forbidden to continue to practise there. He had set up a clinic together with Dr Eslon, who had become an admirer of his treatment methods. The Parisian medical establishment called for an investigation into his claims, and a commission which included Benjamin Franklin found that his claims of having discovered and used animal magnetism were unwarranted, and he was judged to be a fraud. But while the commission was right to maintain that his naturalistic interpretation of his treatment method was unwarranted, unscientific or fraudulent, they were quite wrong in dismissing the therapeutic value of his method. They arrived at the rather portentous view that the effect which Mesmer achieved with his patients had nothing to do with some natural energy but was entirely due to suggestion. They reported that the magnets had no effect and that Mesmer's patients were not cured through the use of magnets, and that therefore the curative effect which Mesmer was able to achieve was entirely due to suggestion. In conclusion they stated that, as the magnets played no part in his patient's recovery and therefore seemed quite irrelevant, Mesmer's methods were unscientific and his claims fraudulent.

It is one of the paradoxes in the development of science that, by its dismissal of Mesmer's claim to have found an empirical basis for his cures, namely animal magnetism, the commission's report drew attention, perhaps without realising it, to the importance of suggestion in therapy, and thereby laid the foundation for scientific investigations of a psychological process whose effects were widely recognised but not understood previously. Indeed, we may say that modern psychotherapy originated with the investigation of the role of suggestion and its employment in what came to be called hypnosis. It was precisely Mesmer's failure to provide proof for his empirical explanations for his cures that focused the attention of others on his therapeutic methods and caused them to investigate the reasons for his successes.

We must remember that the word hypnotism did not yet exist in the medical vocabulary, and it was left to later generations of practitioners and investigators to realise the role of hypnotic suggestion in his cures and to recognise him as the founder of hypnotism. It is open to question whether Mesmer realised that it was the hypnotic states induced in his patients which gave him his curative powers, and whether his so-called empirical explanations were in fact a part of his method of hypnotic induction.

It is interesting also to note that some therapists find the temptation to connect their work and their therapeutic powers with a universal force, which they claim to have discovered, well-nigh irresistible. Another Viennese genius, namely Wilhelm Reich, was also, more recently, determined to find a cosmic energy which would provide empirical evidence for what Freud called the libido. His detailed investigation of the interaction between psychological and physical bodily processes gave a new dimension to psychoanalysis which proved very fruitful for its further development, even though his discoveries are not always recognised. When he began to relate his findings to a force operating in the cosmos, which he called 'cosmic orgone', and tried to prove his theory by the evidence of 'orgone accumulators', he went beyond the constraints of empirical investigations and made the same mistake as Mesmer. Indeed, the similarity between the concepts of 'animal magnetism' and 'cosmic orgone' appears quite unmistakable. Some passages in Mesmer's and Reich's writings show a quite startling similarity. Even if many of their claims stretch one's rational credulity, the hostile reactions which they aroused amongst the experts and the professional establishments and even governments must remain a source of astonishment. Mesmer was expelled from Paris and prevented from continuing his work, and Reich was put in prison, where he died.

But to return to Mesmer and his followers. Perhaps one of the most significant figures in the foundation of psychotherapy was one of Mesmer's closest followers, Armand de Puységur. What he described as the state of somnambulism was similar to the present concept of hypnotic trance, when patients can open their eyes, walk about and speak and respond to the hypnotist's suggestions. He would ask his patients to verbalise their problems during the somnambulistic state, giving details about the origins and causes of their symptoms and, in turn, receive and respond to suggestions.

Among subsequent researchers into hypnotism, Elliotson,

Braid, Esdaile, Liébeault, Bernheim, Charcot and Breuer were probably the most significant. They took up Mesmer's work, and developed it to produce new ideas and new methods. Braid was chiefly impressed as a surgeon by the powers of hypnosis, which make it possible to carry out operations on patients during the hypnotic state. James Esdaile used the hypnotic trance state as an analgesic in surgery. His work was responsible for a widespread employment of hypno-surgery, and despite the advent of chemical analgetics since his time there are still certain occasions when hypnosis can provide a useful alternative.

Bernheim recognised that suggestion is the main underlying factor in hypnosis. He showed that the causes of hypnotic induction were psychological rather than physical even while hypnotic suggestion can produce profound physiological changes. He employed hypnotic therapy both for psychological as well as psychosomatic disorders with considerable success.

However, it was Charcot and Breuer who were among the first to draw attention to the unconscious mind and had a decisive influence upon the development of Freud's ideas. We must also mention Pierre Janet, who became convinced that under hypnosis the conscious mind undergoes repression and makes it possible for the unconscious to come to the fore and to dominate the mind. He was able to show, with the help of hypnosis, that the symptoms of hysteria were firmly dependent upon certain unconscious thoughts. Janet attributed to hysteria a supposed constitutional incapacity for holding mental processes together – an incapacity which led to a disintegration (dissociation) of mental life.

Psychoanalysis, as Freud pointed out, was not in any way based on the researches of Janet. The decisive factors in its development were the experiments which Freud witnessed in Charcot's clinic and the work of Joseph Breuer.

While Freud was working as a young neurologist in Dr Brücke's laboratory, Dr Breuer told him of the case of Anna O., whom he had been treating for nearly two years. The details of this case captured Freud's imagination, particularly the observation that Anna O's hysterical symptoms could be made to disappear permanently when, under hypnosis the circumstances surrounding their origin were unravelled and thus discharged.

3. FREUD'S ENCOUNTER WITH THE UNCONSCIOUS

Breuer's treatment had enabled him to penetrate deeply into the causation and significance of hysterical symptoms; they uncovered mental processes, forgotten ideas and memories which were shown to have a direct bearing upon her physiological disturbances. Breuer's account of his experience with Fräulein Anna O. was unquestionably a major determinant in arousing Freud's attention and interest in the problem of the psychoneuroses, although the incident apparently lay dormant in his mind for the next few years.

As it turned out, his visit to Charcot brought these interests to the foreground again and proved pivotal to his shift from neurophysiological to psychopathological investigations. As Ernest Jones observed: 'It was assuredly the experience with Charcot in Paris that aroused Freud's interest in hysteria, then in psychopathology in general, and so paved the way for resuscitating Breuer's observations and developing psychoanalysis'. Most of all, however, it was his discovery of hypnosis at Charcot's clinic which had a powerful impact upon Freud's mind. Many years later he wrote that he always liked to refer anyone who doubted the existence of the unconscious to the extraordinary processes that take place under hypnosis. There is no doubt that the phenomena of hypnotic suggestion made him recognise the power of unconscious ideas upon the organic as well as psychological functions.

Charcot, who was a specialist in organic diseases of the nervous system, had become increasingly interested in patients suffering from hysteria. Before he began to investigate these symptoms, physicians had felt that hysteria did not deserve their attention, and patients with this diagnosis were often considered to be malingerers, or worse. Charcot was one of the most brilliant observers and classifiers in all psychiatric-neurological history. In keeping with his extraordinary capacity to connect apparently disparate symptoms into coherent syndromes, he pieced together the various components of hysteria into a single syndrome. Freud observed that: 'The whole trend of his mind leads me to suppose that he can find no rest until he has correctly defined and clarified some phenomenon.' But he added: 'He can sleep quite soundly, however, without having arrived at a satisfactory explanation of that phenomenon.' Charcot recognised hysteria as a mental phenomenon but, while he was aware of certain mental and emotional factors relevant to the disease, he simultaneously leaned heavily upon a concept of an inherent neuropathic tendency. This vacillation between psychological and organic determinants was paralleled by his vacillation between a recognition of the sexual factors and his attempt to show that the neurosis is not necessarily connected with the genital system, as had been thought before. While in most cases he recognised the linkage between sexuality and hysterical neurosis, he did not take the next step, namely, to implicate sexual feelings or drives in his theoretical formulations, although he took them for granted in his clinical descriptions and case histories.

His chief contribution to the study of hysteria, besides his detailed descriptions of its manifestations, was to show that the symptoms of the disease could be induced by suggestions given to a patient while he was in a hypnotic trance, and that, furthermore, the symptoms induced in this manner, as well as genuine hysteric symptoms, could be removed by hypnotic suggestion.

Freud recollected that he was particularly impressed by the fact that Charcot could produce paralyses and contractions by hypnotic suggestion and by the fact that such artificially produced symptoms showed, down to the smallest detail, the same features as spontaneous attacks.

Despite Charcot's adherence to the physical-neurological approach to hysteric manifestations, as a clinician he assumed the role of a psychotherapist. He used hypnosis, suggestion, exhortation and environmental and transference manipulation, i.e. he frequently used his charismatic personality on patients. He was, as we have remarked, perfectly aware of psychological factors and described them in clinical papers, which Freud heard and which he remembered when he came to develop his own ideas. Thus the visit to Paris helped Freud significantly to break out of the neurophysiological strait-jacket in his approach to psychiatry – a strait-jacket which at that time was equated with sound science and which, in our own time, once again claims exclusive dominion in 'empirical psychiatry'. It was not Charcot the neurologist but Charcot the psychotherapist who helped Freud towards a clearer understanding of the factors responsible for neurotic diseases. He wrote: 'Monsieur Charcot was the first to teach us that to explain the hysterical neuroses we must appeal to psychology.'

Although Charcot had no systematic way of conceptualising or explaining the facts of emotional traumas, he had a startling perception of their importance in hysteria, whatever his theoretical statements about the neurophysiological predispositions may have been. By 1885 he seemed convinced that hysteria required mental treatment: 'We have here a psychical affliction; it is therefore by a mental treatment that we must hope to modify it.'

The many similarities between Charcot's hypnotic methods and Breuer's treatment of Anna O. prompted Freud to mention the case to Charcot, but much to his disappointment Charcot seemed unimpressed and failed to share his enthusiasm about Breuer's discovery.

In the autumn of 1886 Freud returned to Vienna and settled down as a specialist in nervous diseases. He turned once more to Breuer's observations and made him tell him more about the case of Anna O. This patient had been a young girl of unusual education and gifts who had fallen ill while she was nursing her father, of whom she was devotedly fond. When Breuer took over her case it presented a variegated picture of paralysis, with contrac-tions, inhibitions and states of mental confusion. A chance observation showed him that the patient could be relieved of these clouded states of consciousness if she was induced to express in words the affective fantasy by which she was at the moment dominated. From this discovery, Breuer arrived at a new method of treatment. He put her into deep hypnosis and made her tell him each time what it was that was oppressing her mind. After the attacks of depressive confusion had been overcome in this way, he employed the same procedure for removing her inhibitions and physical disorders. In her waking state the girl could no more describe than other patients how her symptoms had arisen, and she could discover no link between them and any experiences of her life. In hypnosis she immediately revealed the missing connection. When the patient recalled certain situations which were highly emotionally charged under hypnosis, with a free expression of emotion, the symptom was abolished and did not return. By this procedure Breuer succeeded, after long and painful efforts, in relieving his patient of all symptoms.

The immediate question came to Freud's mind whether it was possible to generalise from what had been found in a single case. The state of things which Breuer had discovered seemed to Freud to be of so fundamental a nature that he could not believe it could fail to be present in every case of hysteria if it had been proved to occur in a single one. But as he observed: 'The question could only be decided by experience.' He began to repeat Breuer's investigations with his own patients. After observing for several years that Breuer's findings were invariably confirmed in every case of hysteria that was accessible to hypnotic treatment, and after having accumulated a considerable amount of material in the shape of observations analogous to his, he proposed to him that they should issue a joint publication. In 1893 they issued a preliminary paper *On the Psychical Mechanism of Hysterical Phenomena*, and in 1895 there followed the book *Studies in Hysteria*. Breuer called their method 'cathartic'; its therapeutic aim was to make it possible for the emotional drive, which had got stuck in the wrong lines and was, as such, responsible for the symptoms, to be directed onto the normal path, along which it could obtain discharge. Their book laid stress upon the significance of the life of the emotions and on the importance of distinguishing between mental acts which are unconscious and those which are conscious; it introduced a dynamic factor which supposed that a symptom arises through the damming up of an affect, and an economic factor regarding that same symptom as the product or equivalent of a quantity of energy which would otherwise have been employed in some other way.

In his rapidly increasing experience, Freud learnt that it was not just any kind of emotional excitation that was in action behind the phenomena of the neurosis but habitually one of a sexual nature – whether it was a current sexual conflict or the effect of earlier sexual experiences. As he recalled, 'I was not prepared for this conclusion and my expectation played no part in it, for I had begun my investigations of neurotics quite unsuspectingly.'

Under the influence of his surprising discoveries, Freud took a momentous step. He went beyond the domain of hysteria and began to investigate the sexual life of the so-called neurasthenics, who used to visit him in large numbers.

Having become convinced of the importance of sexuality as a precipitating factor in the development of hysteria and neurasthenia, he increasingly came to ask by what mechanism the sexual memories came to be forgotten, blocked from discharge, and converted into symptoms. While hypnotism had been of immense help in the cathartic treatment by widening the field of the patient's consciousness and putting within his reach knowledge which the patient did not possess in his waking life, Freud found the method restricting as it showed obvious limitations in the degree to which it was applicable to various patients. Freud visited Bernheim in Nancy in order to improve the method and to learn more about it, and there witnessed an experiment which proved to be of great importance in the clarification of the problem of forgetting or of the problem of why patients managed to forget some of the most powerful emotional experiences. When one of Bernheim's subjects awoke from the state of somnambulism, he seemed to have lost all memory of what had happened while he was in that state. Bernheim maintained that the memory was present all the same; and if he insisted on the subject remembering, if he asserted that the subject knew it all and only had to say it, and if at the same time he laid his hand on the subject's forehead, then the forgotten memories used in fact to return, hesitatingly at first but eventually in a flood and with complete clarity.

Freud decided that he would act in the same way as Bernheim when he made his patients recall memories they had forgotten after their hypnosis. He reflected that his patients must in fact 'know' all the things which had hitherto only been made accessible to them in hypnosis, and he drew an analogy between events forgotten after hypnosis and the forgotten events that play an important part in the formation of symptoms. Assurances and encouragement on his part, assisted perhaps by the touch of his hand, would, he thought, have the power of forcing the forgotten facts into consciousness. By one of those insights which enables genius to go beyond the plodding experiments of ordinary talent he came to equate in his mind the events under hypnosis which afterwards appeared to be forgotten with the traumas of neurotics that are normally forgotten or repressed from consciousness.

He drew the conclusion that the urges and desires which for some reason came to be repressed could only find expression in symptoms, that in fact the symptom appears in place of the desire not expressed. However, the urges repressed continue to seek entry into consciousness, the action denied still craves expression. In hysterics, emotional drive is converted into somatic forms of expression (conversion hysteria). If, therefore, the defences against the emotional drive, the repressive agent, could be removed, then symptoms would cease to be necessary and would disappear. This had been made possible to a considerable extent by Breuer's method of catharsis by means of hypnotism. But Freud was determined to do without the aid of hypnosis for two reasons: first, because in spite of a course of instruction with Bernheim at Nancy, he did not succeed in inducing hypnosis in a sufficient number of cases, and secondly, because he was dissatisfied with the therapeutic results of catharsis based on hypnosis. It is true that these results were striking and appeared after a treatment of short duration, but they turned out not to be permanent and to depend too much on the patient's personal relations with the physician.

4. PSYCHOANALYSIS IS BORN

One may consider it lucky for the development of psychoanalysis that Freud was not a particularly good hypnotist. This was probably due to his distaste for the authoritarian method of hypnotic induction prevalent in his time, when the hypnotist adopted what came to be called the role of the paternal superego, imposing his will upon the patient in order to weaken or eliminate his normal ego functions reducing him to a passive responder to the hypnotist's commands. He was also clearly reluctant to become emotionally involved with his patient as this would threaten his independence and his jealously guarded scientific objectivity. In any case, at the turn of the century an emotional intimacy with patients would have been considered inappropriate and practically taboo in patient/doctor relationships. In other words, he had not at that time discovered the important role of transference in therapy, and did not know how to handle its manifestations.

The nineteenth century prudery, which Freud had overcome intellectually with his unflinching and courageous determination to discover the roots and causes of many psychological phenomena, continued to influence his emotional relationships, and the more he learnt about the dynamics of sexual impulses in the aetiology of neuroses, the more he was careful not to allow himself to be in any way affected by them. He neither wished his patients to become too dependent upon him nor to have his independence disturbed by them. It became a hallmark of psychoanalytic practice to maintain an impersonal, unemotional relationship with patients, not to touch them or even shake hands with them, at all times to remain aloof and to be merely a mirror upon whom the patient would project his own fantasies and urges, without any emotional participation by the therapist, not to give advice or much sympathy, to understand without responding, to see patients but not to be seen by them during the analytic hour. There is no doubt that by maintaining his emotional independence and his intellectual freedom to observe the material presented by the patient unrestrained by any personal ties, Freud was enabled to gain new insights into the working of the human psyche and to make theoretical formulations which revolutionised psychology. But by adopting this method Freud also laid the foundation for therapeutic shortcomings which have become increasingly manifest in recent decades due to the emotional sense of isolation which patients experience. The emotional restraints which psychoanalysis imposes upon its practitioners, their impersonal and inhibited attitudes are no longer seen as a virtue but as a denial or rejection of the patient's need for emotional responses. It is something of an anachronism that Victorian prudery with all its restraints and anxieties invades the psychoanalytic setting and fails to meet contemporary expectations of a person-to-person relationship between therapist and patient.

It is true to say that psychoanalysis began with the abandonment of hypnosis as a therapeutic method. What Freud learned from Breuer's method was that the investigation into the causes of an ailment at the same time also served the purpose of its removal. This unusual conjunction was, as Freud maintained, retained in psychoanalysis.

Hypnosis had performed the service of restoring to the patient's memory what he had forgotten, but Freud considered it necessary to find another technique to replace it. However, the means which he first adopted for overcoming the patient's resistance, namely, insisting that the patient must know what is in the back of his mind and encouraging him to remember, which he learned from Bernheim, proved to be too much of a strain on both sides. It also seemed open to certain obvious criticisms, particularly, that the therapist imposes his ideas upon the patient and tries to make him believe whatever the therapist considers to be the correct answer or solution. This was repugnant to Freud and filled him with a kind of horror that psychoanalysis should be accused of being a suggestive therapy and thus harm its scientific credibility. In any case he had learned that it is only by the patient's own ability to reconstruct and re-experience the cause and the development of his symptoms that they can be made to disappear. Any extraneous suggestion may have a passing effect but can rarely be considered a solution in the long run. He therefore adopted another method which was in one sense its opposite. Instead of urging the patient to say something upon some particular subject, he now asked him to abandon himself to a process of free association (*freier Einfall*) – that is, to say whatever came into his head, while ceasing to give any conscious direction to his thought. It was essential, however, that he should bind himself to report literally everything that occurred to his self-perception, and not to give way to critical objections which sought to put certain associations on one side on the ground that they were not sufficiently important or that they were irrelevant or that they were altogether meaningless. The complete candour on the patient's part in reporting his thoughts was the precondition of the whole analytic treatment. Freud pledged his patients to refrain from any conscious reflection and to abandon themselves, in a state of quiet concentration, to follow the ideas which occurred to them spontaneously (involuntarily). They were to communicate these ideas even if they felt objections to doing so, if, for instance, the thoughts seemed too disagreeable, too senseless, too unimportant or lewd and shameful.

Freud was led to the choice of free association as a means of investigating the forgotten unconscious material by an expectation that the so-called 'free' association would prove in fact to be unfree, since, when all conscious considerations had been discarded, the ideas that emerged would seem to be determined by the unconscious material. He realised that the drives and urges, which for some reason or other were repressed and thereby converted into symptoms, were pushing toward expression, seeking entry into consciousness and motor discharge; the impulses and thoughts which were repressed nevertheless still crave for expression.

Having abandoned hypnosis, he was highly elated to find that 'the fundamental rule of psychoanalysis', the course of free association, produced a plentiful store of ideas which could put one on the track of what the patient had forgotten. However, he observed that the material did not bring up what had actually been forgotten, but it brought up such plain and numerous hints about it, that, with the help of a certain amount of supplementing and interpreting, the analyst would be able to reconstruct the forgotten material from it. Thus free association together with the art of interpretation performed the same function as had previously been performed by hypnotism. However, it looked as though his work had been made much more difficult and complicated than he first thought; but the inestimable gain was that an insight was now obtained into an interplay of forces which had been concealed from the observer by the hypnotic state. It became evident that the work of uncovering what had been pathogenically forgotten had to struggle against a constant and very intense resistance. The critical objections, which the patient raised in order to avoid communicating the ideas which occurred to him, were themselves manifestations of this resistance. A consideration of the phenomena of resistance led to one of the corner-stones of the psychoanalytic theory of the neurosis, the theory of repression. The conflicts which occurred during free association provided new insights into the nature of forces that were struggling against each other. Repression invariably proceeded from the patient's conscious personality, and took its stand on aesthetic and ethical motives; the impulses that were subjected to repression were those of selfishness and cruelty, and, above all, sexual impulses, often of the crudest and most forbidden kind. Thus the symptoms were a substitute for forbidden satisfactions, and the illness seemed to correspond to an incomplete subjugation of the immoral side of human beings.

The 'material' produced by free association showed the enormous part played in mental life by sexual urges and fantasies, and led to a detailed study of the nature and development of the sexual drive. Freud discovered that the experiences and conflicts of the first years of childhood play an unsuspectedly important part in the individual's development, and leave behind them ineffaceable consequences. This led to the discovery of infantile sexuality which had hitherto been fundamentally overlooked by science. As the sexual drive is manifested from the earliest age in a person's life, in physical reactions as well as in mental attitudes, the concept of what is sexual had itself to be corrected and widened in a manner which could be justified by the evolution of the sexual instinct. Psychoanalysis gradually acquired a theory which appeared to give a satisfactory account of the origin, meaning and purpose of neurotic symptoms: emphasis on instinctual life, on mental dynamics, on the fact that even the apparently most obscure and arbitrary mental phenomena invariably have a meaning and a causation, the theory of psychic conflict and of the pathogenic nature of repression, the view that symptoms are substitute satisfactions and the recognition of the aetiological importance of sexual life. Among the affective attitudes of childhood, the complicated emotional relation of children to their parents – what is known as the Oedipus complex – came into prominence. It became ever clearer to Freud that this was the nucleus of every case of neurosis, and that furthermore the patient transferred his Oedipus complex, his emotional fixations on his parents and his sexual conflicts to his analyst. This came to be known as transference and is a fundamental concept for psychoanalytical theory and technique alike. Freud, at first with some surprise but then with a sense of recognition of its inevitability, found that psychoanalytic theory of the neurosis contained a number of things which ran counter to accepted opinions and inclinations and which were calculated to provoke astonishment, repugnance and scepticism in outsiders.

In 1914 he wrote: 'Any line of enquiry which recognises repression and transference facts and takes them as a starting-point of its work has a right to call itself psychoanalysis, even though it arrives at results other than my own.' We must also include the unconscious, infantile sexuality, the libido theory, the Oedipus complex and the division of the mental apparatus into id, ego and superego and their dynamic interaction as fundamental to psychoanalytic theory. We might say that any method and theory which gives full recognition to these factors can be called psychoanalytic, even if it does not strictly adhere to free association as a therapeutic tool.

2 The Limitations of Language

1. THE PRE-VERBAL WORLD OF THE MIND: BEFORE WORDS

Like many analysts before me (and many patients), I became aware of the limitations of free association and the conjectural nature of interpreting the psychic material produced. Whereas it was useful for the analyst to understand the nature of repression and resistance which impede his patient's progress, the analyst's understanding all too often was unable to overcome those resistances. Freud used to send postcards to his disciples in which he indicated the length of the treatment to be expected in certain types of neurosis, usually ranging from a few weeks to six months. Since those early days analytic treatment has become ever more lengthy, and a number of years is now considered normal. One may ask why this should be so. Does it merely reflect Freud's over-optimism or does it expose an inherent flaw in his method? We might say that Freud clung to free association as an essential part of psychoanalytic therapy in order to keep his system intact, as any major deviation from it would have allowed the resistances of our culture and people's prejudices to undermine the gains for which he had so laboriously worked. He probably felt that any chink in the armour of his scientific edifice would be exploited by his enemies. On the other hand it is equally probable that he could not think of any better method. In his later years he maintained that even if the therapeutic results of psychoanalysis proved to be disappointing, its aim went beyond mere therapeutic efficiency, its chief purpose being the extension of our understanding of the psyche and the improvement of people's ability to understand themselves and their fellow men.

While I always sympathised with this view, I became more and more convinced that if the method of free association failed to provide the results which were expected from it, it was not enough merely to restrain one's therapeutic expectations, one's 'furor therapeuticus', as Freud put it. I considered it a matter of commonsense that the method had to be changed in order to improve clinical results and facilitate patients' ability to overcome their resistances and obtain a better understanding of the hidden world of the unconscious. There is no doubt that the laborious method of free association enabled Freud to gain insight into quite unexpected areas of the human psyche, which he would not have discovered without it. However, it seems necessary to improve the tool without losing sight of or destroying the edifice which has already been constructed.

A close examination of the limitations of Freud's therapeutic tool may point to a way in which it can be improved:

1) While the patient's free associations have made it possible for psychoanalysts to arrive at certain insights into unconscious processes and the laws which govern them, it does not enable patients to experience the unconscious directly.

2) As free association depends upon verbal expression, it cannot communicate psychic experiences which occur in infancy before verbal communication is established.

3) Psychoanalytic therapy requires the analyst to interpret the material presented to him in the course of free association. These interpretations may be correct or not,

and even if correct are all too often not recognised as relevant by the patients.

4) The element of surprise and even shock, so important in psychoanalytic procedure, is largely reduced in our time, when a wide range of sexual urges and perversions have become common knowledge. This has led to the phenomenon of intellectual defence mechanisms: 'We know all about it, and therefore do not consider that we have discovered something new and unknown to us.'

5) The psychoanalytic method is unable to penetrate to the physiological disturbances which accompany psychic conflicts and perpetuate them. Every psychological process has its physiological counterpart – psyche and soma presenting an indivisible whole – and as long as the analysis does not release a patient from his bodily tensions it cannot release him from his neurosis.

6) The restraints placed upon the therapist in communicating his feelings and emotional reactions in therapy produce a sense of isolation anxiety in patients from which they had suffered in the first place. In the analyst also the enforced inhibition of emotional and intellectual communication restricts his experience of empathy which is of pre-eminent importance for his understanding of his patient's psychic processes.

As it is impossible to arrive at a direct experience of the unconscious by means of free association, the analyst has to interpret the verbal communications of his patients and reconstruct the forgotten events in a patient's life which are responsible for his neurotic conflicts and symptoms. However, interpretation, whether it be a science or an art, becomes very problematical if we realise that the words uttered in the course of free association must not be confused with their real meaning. The narrations of the patient frequently hide the psychological content which lies behind them, they are not only ambiguous but frequently are themselves agents of repression. The material presented to the analyst, namely the patient's words, do not express or reveal the historical truth about the origin of symptoms but often are meant to mislead and divert attention away from the very conflicts, the traumas, fears and fixations from which the patient suffers.

2. REVISIONISTS: DIVERTING ATTENTION AWAY FROM THE UNCONSCIOUS

While it is fairly easy to observe a person's manifest behaviour and to hear his words, it is not so easy to understand their real meaning and to discover their unconscious roots. In view of the difficulty psychoanalysts experience in getting their patients to remember and re-experience their unconscious traumas, they have increasingly become preoccupied with the processes of transference and countertransference to a point where the detailed analysis of the patient-therapist relationship has become like an obsession. In therapeutic practice as well as in clinical writings attention has shifted away from areas which Freud regarded as the focal points of psychoanalytic theory and practice: the libido theory, infantile sexuality and the unconscious. Many analysts no longer consider them to be essential issues. They claim that modern psychoanalysis has broken loose from the constraints of orthodoxy and has developed new conceptual frameworks, such as ego psychology, interpersonal relation therapy and, latterly, interactional therapy.

Among the most important advocates of the new or revisionist schools of psychoanalysis we can name H S Sullivan, Heinz Hartmann, Carl Rogers, Erich Fromm, Karen Horney, W R D Fairbairn, W R Bion, Harry Guntrip, and to some extent, as far as attention to ego processes is concerned, Anna Freud. Melanie Klein is in many respects different for she claimed to have delved deeper than Freud into the psychology of infants, where indeed she made many new discoveries, even though her attempts at systemisation are rather contrived. We must also mention

D W Winnicott who, following Melanie Klein, gave much useful information about the infant's experiences of the mothering processes.

Most of the new schools attempt to liberate the analyst/patient relationship from the rigid constraints which orthodoxy has imposed upon it, where the analyst had to act as the impersonal, objective observer, a non-person, so to speak, in order to present the patient with a mirror upon which he could project his unconscious fantasies without being disturbed by considerations of the analyst's personality. The orthodox analyst is not supposed to respond emotionally in any way, not touch his patient, shake hands with him or talk about himself, in short, he must not engage in what is normally considered polite or well-mannered behaviour. But by negating his own personality, he does not acknowledge the patient as a person but merely as a victim of neurotic disturbances.

It is, of course, a significant factor in psychoanalytic therapy that the emotional interaction between patient and analyst is a matter of great sensitivity and importance. As the patient is expected to reveal all his innermost and closely guarded secrets, his desires, urges, traumas and fears, he desperately needs to know how they are received by another person. Having given up his ego defences, and exposing himself to the analyst he becomes vulnerable and dependent upon him and has to know how he reacts emotionally as well as intellectually. By being expected to give up his defences the patient becomes defenceless, so to speak; will the analyst react in the manner expected, will he conform to the judging and punishing superego or the rejective or indifferent mother- or father-figure which the patient has carried in his mind all along, or will he be reassured that his anxieties and embarrassments are no longer necessary? He thus becomes extremely sensitive to the analyst's personality. The impersonal attitude, the apparent indifference towards the patient's gestures of gratitude or tokens of love frequently reinforce his sense of being unwanted or rejected, and I have seen many examples of the anxiety and disorientation which such therapeutic attitudes have produced.

Of course a close observation of the way in which the patient transfers his early relationships with his parents, siblings and other individuals upon whom he was emotionally dependent, how he transfers his complexes, fears and conflicts upon the analyst is an important part of therapy, but it does not have to take place in an impersonal, cold and unsympathetic manner. Such attitudes, as I have said, frequently produce the impression of an authoritarian, all-knowing, judgmental adversary. In order to produce a 'positive transference', which, Freud long ago recognised as being of tremendous help in the therapeutic process, one has to show a measure of 'positive counter-transference' to the patient.

Sympathy and affection does not in a well-balanced analyst disturb his capacity of understanding and objective assessment of his patient's mental processes. The opposite, in fact, is true. We can assume that analysts are after all persons in their own right, however surprising this may seem. Indeed, they are frequently quite eccentric and even neurotic, however well they have managed to cope due to their own psychoanalysis; they have in many respects strong personalities and opinions, and the rule that they have to appear as some kind of a non-person and not show any emotional reactions in the consulting room produces inhibitions and frequently hidden anxieties in the analyst which can communicate themselves to his patients. Having to hide their personalities and opinions and not being allowed to reveal their emotions has the effect of stultifying their capacity of empathy, which is of singular importance in the therapeutic process. As Leonardo da Vinci has said: 'We cannot understand a thing unless we love it.'

However, while orthodoxy knows full well that even analysts have feelings, it maintains that they must not interfere in the analytic process and, if they do, have to be ruthlessly analysed. This is called the counter-transference, a process which has acquired a pejorative meaning. It is true that unresolved complexes and fixations in the analyst if transferred upon the patient can produce blind spots in understanding, wrong interpretations and misjudgments, but it is also true that the inhibitions imposed upon the analyst frequently make him anxious and re-evoke his complexes. Freud himself did not allow himself, or simply could not bear, to be subjected to the rules which became orthodoxy. He would frequently express his opinions on all kinds of matters, he could not hide his personality but had profound intuitive understanding of his patients' psyche and empathy with them. In fact one can say that he broke all the rules which later became the hallmark of psychoanalysis.

The revisionist schools have attempted to open new pathways to a more liberal attitude in psychoanalysis. Many amongst them pay more attention to the patient's personality and show some interest and respect for his values and judgments. They also tend to consider social and political conditions, which Freud is accused of having steadfastly ignored. There is no doubt in my mind that some of these movements have contributed much that is of value and have extended the scope of psychoanalytic investigations. Sullivan and Fromm have been the precursors of what is sometimes called humanistic psychology, and one should not forget Alfred Adler's important contributions in this area. However, orthodox Freudians tend to accuse these movements of being carried away by ethical considerations or social philosophies and of shying away from the fearless and perhaps somewhat ruthless investigations of the unconscious. It is true that by and large these movements have tended to minimise the importance of the unconscious and of infantile sexuality in their theories and in their practice. However this may be, orthodox or liberal, conservative or progressive, scientific or humanistic, they all depend in their therapy upon the art of interpretation of patients' associations, whether it be of the free-floating kind or dream interpretations or the interpretation of resistance and of the transference, of behavioural peculiarities such as over-politeness, or hostility, errors or accidents. Interpretation is after all the therapeutic method which they all share. The problem of arriving at correct interpretations remains, and it is no wonder that sooner or later schools have developed which focus their attention upon the analysis of the words spoken by the patient, for it is after all words which provide the material which the analyst has to operate with.

3. ANALYSING WORDS: A POST-FREUDIAN OBSESSION

A large number of studies have appeared in recent years devoted to a painstaking analysis of the words spoken by patients, and psychoanalytic linguistics has acquired a cult status. Not only in France but also in Anglo-Saxon countries a preoccupation with semantics is seen as the latest fashion in the sharpening of the tools in the psychoanalytic armoury, a sort of obligation for any analyst who would consider himself up to date. However, these analysts of language, in their pride of having found the right tool for the clarification of the meaning behind the patient's words and narratives, have become trapped in their own words and have reduced them to verbiage. They are caught up in almost ritual incantations of phrases such as structuralism and post-structuralism, deconstructionism and post-deconstructionism, signifiers, signified and signification, which are paraded as some kind of latest wisdom in a merry-go-round of fundamentally meaningless phrases. The researchers into the meaning of words have come to use words without meaning; Lacan, Foucault, Ricoeur, Derrida, Pontalis and Laplanche in France are leaders of this fashion, but they have not advanced our understanding of the human psyche nor have they improved therapeutic methods. What they have done is to draw attention away from the unconscious processes to a study of verbal behaviour, to an investigation of the externals which the patient presents in his consulting hour. But his words and his narrative are a very inadequate manifestation of his psychic processes. After all, the words we pronounce, particularly under the stress of anxiety and inhibition, reveal only a small part of our mental experience, and taking the words as if they were the full expression of what goes on in the mind, mistaking them as the equivalent of a person's thoughts, flattens the multi-dimensional complexities and richness of our mental processes. The assumption that the mind is in the words and we only have to study words in order to understand the mind has become one of the self-impoverishing fatuities/vacuities of modern philosophy trapped in linguistic analysis. And the psychoanalysts, who have followed the fashion of linguistic analysis, which has dominated philosophy for too long and has led to a dead-end, practically destroying philosophy in our time, are threatening to do the same to psychoanalysis.

Let me quote a passage from Paul Ricoeur to illustrate what I mean:

'Today we are in search of a comprehensive philosophy of language to account for the multiple functions of the human act of signifying and for their interrelationships... We have at our disposal a symbolic logic, an exegetical science, an anthropology, and a psychoanalysis, and, perhaps for the first time, we are able to encompass in a single question the problem of the unification of human discourse. The very progress of the afore-mentioned disciplines has both revealed and intensified the dismemberment of that discourse. Today the unity of human language poses a problem.' *

Ricoeur had the title of 'philosopher of integral language' bestowed upon him as the man 'able to achieve a comprehensive philosophy about the human mind as reflected in language'. Not a bad example of mystification parading as exactitude!

But it is probably Lacan who is the best known exponent of this school. He claimed that language is 'the vehicle to

---

* S H Clark *Paul Ricoeur* (Routledge, 1990)

express the unconscious', and that 'it is at the level of language that the problem exists. Language is the only communication we know; there is no unconscious except for the speaking being'. He has said many cryptic things in his writings and in his lectures, but what chiefly characterises them is the lack of any logical connection and a profound obscurantism. I have often wondered why it is that a people as intelligent as the French could be led to admire a writer whom they obviously could not understand, as is shown by a special two-year course at Lyons University on 'How to read Lacan'.

Apart from the puzzling phenomenon of Lacan, who surely was a prime candidate for the injunction 'Physician heal thyself', the analysts of psychoanalytic language endeavour to find a key to the hidden areas of the psyche by the endless definition of the meaning of words, but by focusing their studies upon words they lose the capacity to perceive or understand the patient's subjective experiences. Just as words often hide from ourselves and from others what we really mean, so the meaning of neurotic symptoms, which is the proper field of psychoanalytic investigation, has become increasingly hidden to the exponents of modernism (or is it post-modernism, or post-deconstructionism, etc?). Psychoanalytic linguistics has become a special reserve of academics, some of whom have no actual experience of working with patients. They rarely encounter patients' emotional conflicts, their anxieties, pains, hopes, illusions and disillusions, and make abstract studies of what words ought to mean and attempt to produce a system of definitions and rules which ought to enable the analyst to understand the verbal material presented to him. They frequently focus their attention on Freud's writings (producing scores of books on 'How to read Freud') rather than on the patient's experiences as he struggles to express them with the limited means of his vocabulary. Indeed, it must be obvious to any experienced psychoanalyst that the vocabulary which is available to the patient can only express in a very limited way the wealth of his emotions, fantasies and feelings. This does not only apply to neurotic or psychotic patients but is a common characteristic of humanity. Einstein once remarked: 'I do not understand what modern philosophers try to prove with their emphasis upon language, for do we not all experience the difficulty of finding words to express what we feel and think and frequently are unable to do so.'

Language, after all, is one of the many forms by which we communicate our emotional and spiritual experiences: dance, music, painting, sculpture, as well as gestures and postures, usually spontaneously or artificially as in mime, are actually other, more fundamental means of expression, sometimes more profound than words. And, indeed, the analyst, if he is worth his salt, does not merely listen to words spoken, he also observes his patient's gestures, his bodily postures, and his facial expressions in conjunction with what he says. If he is a really good therapist and naturally gifted for his job, he is capable of empathy with his patient and experience a wide range of pre-verbal communications, almost a kind of telepathy, which enables him to become intuitively aware of his patient's state of mind.

3 The Language of the Body: Reich and Vegetotherapy

'We comprehend the expressive movements and the emotional expressions of another living organism on the basis of the identity of our emotions and those of all living beings.'

Wilhelm Reich

1. THE UNITY OF PSYCHE AND SOMA

It is common knowledge that emotional experiences such as fear or anger, pleasure or anxiety evoke bodily reactions, and the human face in particular expresses a wide range of emotions. There is no doubt that there is a language of the body which often reveals much about a person's state of mind. I made it a habit not merely to listen to what patients are saying but also to look at their movements, their postures and gestures. But while I consider it important in a therapeutic encounter not only to listen but also to look and observe, there is also a form of perception which is not limited to our conscious observations but extends to preconscious, subliminal, intuitive impressions, and they evoke our emotional response which we call empathy. The Victorians spoke of radiations emanating from people, and certain photographs have been made in recent years purporting to show these radiations. While these things encounter considerable scientific scepticism, we can all experience sensations of coldness or depression which pervade the atmosphere around some individuals, even if we are not looking particularly carefully. Who has not experienced an air of elation or lightness and feelings of pleasure in the companionship of others? We take these things for granted and some people are particularly sensitive to them. A kind of artistic sensitivity, an openness to intuitive responses, is a quality of considerable value in a therapist, and indeed it can be considered to be even more important than the rational effort of understanding based upon his theoretical models. All too often I have met people who had long terms of psychoanalysis of the Freudian or Jungian or even Kleinian school who assured me that they had learned a lot about those psychologies but little about themselves, and that their therapists did a lot of interpretation but did not really show much real understanding. But in order to empathise with the emotional expressions of his patients the therapist must not block his own emotional expression, particularly from himself, and be free at least to some extent to communicate it to his patients. I well remember an occasion when a patient sat opposite me in a very blocked, tense and depressed state, and I could feel his tension. After about half an hour I jumped up and started to move about, saying it's all very well for him to be tight and tense, he is used to it but I am not. This was quite spontaneous, but at that moment I also felt that it would not do him any harm to notice my reaction and to let him know that I was aware of what he felt. Indeed, the patient looked astounded, but then he grinned and said he quite understood my reaction and started to loosen his body and move about a little. This did not cure anything but it enhanced his trust in me.

Apart from gestures and involuntary postures which express emotions such as fear, anger or sorrow occasioned by actual events, we can recognise permanent expressions in face and body which are characteristic of a person and reflect some deep-seated psychological traits. We can speak of a person's character as the predominance of certain emotional attitudes which become more or less fixed. We thus encounter emotional expressions which are reactive, responses to current and actual events, and those which we can consider to be innate or chronic.

However, emotional responses of the body are not merely manifest in a person's outward behaviour, but also involve internal, organic processes, such as occur in the cardio-vascular, circulatory, respiratory and digestive systems. Everybody knows that situations of danger intensify the heart-beat, and that fear can constrain one's breathing, produce dryness of the mouth or tighten one's stomach. While these involuntary reactions are natural and common-place, they can also become chronic or permanent when they reflect a chronic emotional disturbance. When a person's psyche is dominated by an unrelieved state of anxiety or apprehension, unfulfilled desire, guilt and feelings of inadequacy, just to mention a few of the disturbances people are prone to, he will be subjected to muscular and organic disturbances expressing those emotions. It is the task of psychoanalysis to decipher the meaning of those chronic or neurotic muscular or organic disturbances and trace them to their emotional roots.

More than any other psychoanalyst, Wilhelm Reich drew attention to the interaction between psychic and bodily processes, to the unity of psyche and soma, and made it the focus of his investigations. His work falls into four main stages. The first was the period dominated by his concept of character analysis. This developed out of his investigations into patients' resistances during the early twenties when he was supervisor of the Vienna Seminar of Psychoanalytic Therapy. He emphasised the need for systematic resistance analysis as a precondition for enabling the patient to release the repressed psychic material. He developed a concept of an armour that serves as a defence against the libido which is constantly trying to find entrance

BIBL. LONDIN. UNIV.

into consciousness and discharge by physical means. The armour which is part of a person's attempt to master the id manifests itself not only in his psychic conflicts but also in behavioural attitudes. In addition to the analysis of dreams, of free associations, of a patient's slips, and the way he communicates or fails to do so, the way in which the patient speaks, looks at and greets the analyst, the way he lies on the couch, in short, his behaviour and his postures are valuable clues in assessing the resistances against the basic rule.

Reich considered a patient's resistances to be mainly rooted in his character: 'A woman suffering from hysteria will always defend herself in a way expressive of anxiety, while a person suffering from a compulsive neurosis will always defend himself aggressively, no matter what unconscious content is on the verge of breaking through. The character armour is the moulded expression of the defence mechanism chronically embedded in the psychic structure. Because of its origin in the character, we call this constant resistance factor character resistance.' Reich said that the character resistance is expressed not in terms of content but in the way a patient typically behaves, in the manner in which he speaks, walks and gestures, and in his characteristic habits and behaviour.

While in his early work, the period of character analysis, Reich saw the character armour as a psychic defence apparatus and neurotic symptoms as manifestations of blocked and undischarged psychic energy, he came to pay increased attention to the muscular tensions which accompany the mechanisms of defence. Indeed, he found that there is a symbiotic interaction between the psychological and physical processes, that muscular rigidities enact the psychological inhibitions, and he came to speak of armouring as essentially a physiological process. Character armour thus showed itself to be fundamentally identical with muscular hypertension which he called the muscular armour. His concept of 'functional identity' meant that muscular and character attitudes served the same function in the psychic apparatus. Not only are muscular attitudes an expression of psychic attitudes, but psychic attitudes are also influenced by the physical: they influence and enhance each other. Basically they cannot be separated; in their function they are identical.

I have found this concept of psycho-physical identity and their mutual interaction of enormous importance in therapeutic work, where it proved to be correct again and again.

2. EXPANSION AND CONTRACTION

By 1933 Reich's concept of the unity of psychic and somatic functioning had clarified itself in his formulation of the primary antithesis of what he called vegetative life: namely, pleasure (expansion) and anxiety (contraction). The fundamental biological functions of contraction and expansion were applicable to the psychic as well as somatic realm. This formulation led him beyond the study of defence mechanisms as enacted by the musculature to the study of a wide range of organic processes.

He found that anxiety affects not only the peripheral musculature of the face, neck, shoulders, the back, pelvis, legs and feet, but also deeper physiological functions, such as the salivary glands (parched mouth), sweat glands, contraction of the arteries with its effect upon the circulatory system and the heart, the respiratory functions, the digestive tract from the oesophagus to rectum, contractions of the bladder musculature, inhibition of the blood supply to the female sex organs, producing dry vaginae and vaginal contractions and reduction of sexual sensations; in the case of male sex organs a tightening of the musculature of the scrotum, reduction of glandular functions and decrease of blood supply into the penis, inhibiting its erective capacity.

Character analysis thus developed into vegetotherapy. While he intended at first to combine the work concerning the psyche with attention to the physical apparatus, his emphasis increasingly shifted from the psychological to the physiological realm. Vegetotherapy aimed at dissolving the muscular armour and the contractive processes of the body, making it possible for psychobiological energies, particularly the sexual and aggressive drives which were blocked, to be discharged.

Reich claimed that by releasing the patient from his muscular tensions, unconscious traumatic experiences would enter consciousness and his libido energies would be set free, allowing the previously rigid and armoured organism to be capable of natural expression; the patient's sexual anxieties and inhibitions would be replaced by orgastic potency.

It was Reich's immense contribution towards our understanding of human pathology that he drew our attention to the intimate relationship between psychic and bodily processes, the unity of psyche and soma which psychoanalysis could only ignore to its disadvantage. He laid the foundations for psychosomatic medicine and moreover showed that neurotic disturbances are not merely of a psychological nature but are also accompanied by somatic disturbances, in fact that every psychoneurosis is psychosomatic.

But he went further. He postulated a biological energy, a life energy which permeates all living things and which, if blocked, produces contractions, tensions and anxieties. He replaced the concept of libido with a concept of bioenergy (orgone), which could be observed empirically and provide opportunities for exact scientific investigations which Freud's libido theory could not provide. Indeed, he took great pride in having made it possible to transform psychology into a natural science. His concept of the 'bione' as a specific bioenergy operating in the cells of the human body was one of the most courageous incursions into the study of fundamental life functions. It promised to provide new insights into the creation of cancer cells, as well as making it possible to measure the bioenergetic radiations which emanate from a person's periphery.

He defined biones as microscopic vesicles charged with orgone energy (energy vesicles) which can be produced from organic and inorganic material. They develop, he maintained, spontaneously in soil or as in cancer from disintegrating tissues. In his book *Die Bione* (1938) he provides what he considered to be experimental evidence for the natural organisation of living substances. But his extraordinarily fertile mind would not be content till he found a universal life force which operates in the psychic, the biological as well as the physical realm, and he called it the cosmic orgone energy. He regarded his conception of a cosmic energy not merely as a theoretical hypothesis but as a physical entity which morcover could be manipulated in order to provide fresh energy to human organisms which had been depleted of it. He built orgone boxes which were meant to accumulate concentrated orgone energy, which a patient by sitting in them would absorb into his body and find himself revitalised, his life-affirming powers improved and his psychic and somatic disturbances resolved.

But apart from his investigations into the impact of the cosmic energy upon the human organism, he increasingly became preoccupied with the problems of the physical world. He designed cloud busters which could send orgone energy into clouds and produce rain, he developed a concept of DOR (death orgone), which he held to be responsible for arid and decaying natural environment. In short, in the latest stage of his work he developed what he called the science of orgone physics and cosmic orgone engineering. He even designed an orgone motor. (There is much argument among his followers about what happened to this design). He called himself the discoverer of the cosmic life force and felt aggrieved that the official world did not give full recognition to his spectacular discovery.

This is a very condensed summary of his theoretical and scientific development with its ascension to new insights into the human condition and the nature of the universe. Many have considered the development of his ideas not so much an ascendance but a descendance to the realm of mystical speculation, even bordering upon manic fantasies. But in his problematical intellectual journey Reich has made many important discoveries which are a lasting contribution to psychology and if viewed with a critical mind can encourage investigations into new fields.

While on a theoretical level I assume that there is a cosmic force or energy that pervades the universe, scientific evidence must surely be provided by astronomers and cosmologists. Whether the energy released in the 'big bang' continues to pervade the known universe and can be held responsible for the formation and behaviour of galaxies, the stars and planets, and whether we ourselves and all organic life on this planet are the embodiment of this energy, is something I like to speculate about but would have to look for the scientists in the above fields to provide evidence. Like Mesmer, Reich went wrong when he claimed to have found sufficient scientific evidence for the universal energy, which Mesmer called animal magnetism, rather than leaving it as an important, somewhat metaphysical speculation which might stimulate further research. His claim of having found conclusive proof has aroused widespread resentment and has foreclosed further interest among scientists.

While I have found no evidence for an atmospheric or cosmic orgone, I consider many of Reich's insights extremely useful and have received ample evidence for them in my therapeutic work. His emphasis upon the unity of psychological and physiological processes, his concept of the armour as a psychic inhibition expressed by muscular contractions, his theory that chronic anxiety finds its counterpart in chronic rigidities and contractions of the body, and the fundamental antithesis between pleasure (expansion) and anxiety (contraction), are an important contribution to our understanding of psychosomatic processes. What he calls emotional expression observable in bodily reflexes, postures and attitudes opens up a new highway to the unconscious and releases the therapist from the limitation of having to depend exclusively upon verbal communication.

Again and again I observed that psychological processes inevitably evoke physiological responses and that chronic psychological disturbances produce physiological reactions of a chronic nature. Neurotic anxieties produce muscular tensions and organic contractions which can lead to respiratory disturbances such as asthma, cardiac and other circulatory diseases, can affect the digestive system, the stomach, the bowels or the colon, or create disturbances of the repro-ductive system, of sexual functions as well as contractions of the spinal column. Even bones and teeth can become affected by profound psychological conflicts. The extraordinary, powerful interaction between psyche and soma inevitably comes as a surprise to our habitual way of thinking, which divides mind and body into apparently two separate systems and evokes considerable resistance among laymen as well as the medical establishment. I have myself at first reacted with considerable astonishment, and even disbelief, to my own observations; but the evidence of my practical work with patients could not be ignored, particularly as many physical afflictions could be made to disappear if their origins were traced to specific psychological causes. However, before I could achieve these results, I had to learn that Reich's claim, that, by dissolving a patient's muscular armour by means of vegetotherapy, his psychic conflicts and traumas would enter consciousness, has not been borne out. I have treated Reichian practitioners, and we had to witness the inadequacy of vegetotherapy. The breakthrough of previously repressed emotions, and their acting out in crying, kicking and biting did not release them from their neurotic disturbances. They still had to confront their repressed psychic processes: vegetotherapy or the various physical treatment methods derived from it had to be combined with psychoanalytical insight therapy.

4 The Highroad to the Unconscious: Hypnosis reconsidered

Again I faced the old problem of the inaccessibility of repressed psychic processes, the immense difficulty of gaining access to the unconscious. Free association was a very slow and unpredictable method, not so much a highroad to the unconscious as a winding country lane that often petered out in forest and field, leading nowhere and leaving the walker lost and bemused. It seemed inevitable to me that one had to search for a more efficient and reliable path, a better constructed road that would lead one to the destination desired. I started thinking again about hypnotism and its ability to produce transformations in a person's mind which facilitate the recall of long forgotten experiences. What seemed particularly important was the hypnotised person's ability not only to remember but also to re-experience the emotions aroused by long forgotten traumas or shocks which in their repressed state found discharge in neurotic symptoms.

The extraordinary feats of memory and the re-experience of past events under hypnosis have been well attested and widely reported. Moreover, it is known that under hypnosis the body can undergo transformations which otherwise would not be possible. Metabolism, heart rate, respiration and vision as well as muscular functions can be made to undergo profound changes. One of the most spectacular feats of strength which can be brought about by hypnosis is often performed on the stage when a hypnotised person is told to lie between two chairs, with his head resting on one chair and his feet on the other while his body is suspended between. I witnessed one such performance many years ago at a military camp entertainment in Aldershot. My young brother, who had acquired considerable skill as a hypnotist, was stationed there as a conscript and was ready to oblige his fellow soldiers who were keen to see him perform some of his 'tricks'. He asked for volunteers to come on to the stage, and of course half of the audience wanted to participate. He kept five or six soldiers and hypnotised them without much ado. He then got one of the hypnotised boys to put his head on one chair and his feet on the other with no additional support, and told him that at the count of five his body would be as rigid and stiff as an iron rod and nothing on earth could bend it. And, indeed, one could see his body becoming rigid, and two soldiers from the audience were asked to stand on him. They were then asked to move and jump about a bit. And the soldiers did so, at first very gingerly, but when they saw that their comrade's body did not bend under their weight their movement became more lively. And still the suspended body did not bend but remained completely rigid and did not show the slightest difficulty in supporting their weight with their army boots. When the soldier was eventually told to get up from the chairs and was de-hypnotised, he was asked whether he felt any pain or any discomfort at all; he was surprised at the question and didn't show any discomfort.

At the same performance my brother also invited two officers on to the stage and asked them to shake hands. He then told them that he was going to tell them a little story and that when he mentioned a certain number they would not be able to separate their hands and would be stuck together however much they tried to separate them. And to the hilarity of the soldiers in the audience, their two officers were unable to let go of each other however much they tried. My brother then simply said, 'Let go!', and much to their relief they could do so.

Such hypnotic phenomena may cause amusement and astonishment but as a psychologist one asks the question about what is actually happening here. It is a question which not only concerns the psychologist but also the neurophysiologist. For, what are the mental processes which enable hypnotised persons to perform acts of strength which would be beyond the capacity of even the most athletic individuals? One is reminded of William James' dictum that we normally only exercise a small proportion of our physical and mental potentials, and it seems that under hypnosis the powers which normally are repressed and kept in reserve are called into action. It is not enough to say that the young man lying between two chairs was a complaisant individual and chose to obey the commands of the hypnotist, as some theoreticians of hypnosis tend to maintain. There is simply no way that a person in his conscious state or by his own free will could perform such feats. At the same time, I am certainly not inclined to talk about some superhuman force or magic at work here. We can say that under hypnosis the individual is called upon to exercise all his (unconscious) potentials and reserves of strength which are not normally available to him.

We have mentioned earlier that hypnotic phenomena play an important part in religions, rituals, in nationalistic fervours and political fanaticism which make people prepared to kill at the command of a leader or king or priest. History is replete with outbreaks of mass hysteria, when people are overwhelmed by palpably irrational fantasies which drive them to acts of violence and cruelty which, if left to their own conscious judgement, they would not consider permissible.

Besides the extraordinary manifestations of muscular power I have mentioned, we can also see transformations of visual perception under the influence of hypnosis. When I began to study psychology I experimented with free association and dream interpretation as well as hypnosis with my fellow students. We presented each other with dreams to be analysed, we left no mistake or slip of the tongue or accident unanalysed. We did not understand much about these things but we were determined to learn from each other and we also hypnotised each other at every possible occasion. On one occasion I was hypnotised and instructed that upon waking up I would look into a mirror and see myself with a golden nose. When I woke up I promptly looked into a mirror conveniently placed at an obvious position for me to see and, indeed, I had a golden nose. There was no sense of illusion or confusion about it. My nose had turned golden. After a moment of intense surprise I became rather anxious about it, for, after all, it is disconcerting to have grown a nose which is quite different from the one which one has been familiar with all one's life. I gave vent to my amazement and concern, but then my fellow students could no longer restrain their laughter and I realised that I was under a post-hypnotic suggestion and the image disappeared. A post-hypnotic suggestion which always arouses much amusement among onlookers is to make the subject upon waking up get hold of an umbrella and open it, and what is particularly interesting is that inevitably the person who opens the umbrella and walks about with it in a room finds plausible justifications for doing so. One is here reminded of psychotics who are always ready, often in the most rational sounding manner, to justify their frequently very bizarre behaviour and fantasies.

Some years ago I was visiting a patient in a hospital when a man was brought in with a heart infarct and close to death. I hypnotised him and told him that his metabolic rate would be greatly reduced, that his heart rate would be down to thirty or so and that he would sleep in this condition for three days and three nights. The idea was to ease the pressure on his heart, on the circulatory and respiratory processes and make it possible for his body to recover. Although the doctors were somewhat alarmed at the continued deep sleep and metabolic state of this patient under hypnosis, they were interested enough to see what effect it would have upon him. Indeed, after three days he woke up much improved and eventually recovered. (This procedure is recognised now and adopted in some hospitals.) Conversely, one can increase the heart beat, induce acute muscular tensions amounting to a paralysis of the limbs and a great number of organic aberrations which are in their appearance indistinguishable from a physical disease.

If one considers that hypnotic suggestions can produce mental and physical aberrations which are similar to neurotic or psychotic symptoms, then one may conclude that a hypnotic suggestion acts in a way similar to a trauma. Having been repressed from consciousness, the trauma continues to operate in the unconscious mind, in the same way as an hypnotic suggestion, and produces psychic and somatic transformations which appear to have no connection with reality and have no meaning but operate with the force of a compulsion as symptoms. When I understood that the golden nose which I saw in the mirror was caused by a post-hypnotic suggestion, it disappeared and I had my own natural nose again. The golden nose could be likened to a neurotic symptom, with the difference that my momentary neurosis was caused by a hypnotic command, whereas a real neurosis is caused by real experiences long forgotten; and if these experiences can be remembered and connected with the symptom, then the symptom can disappear, the chronic obsession transformed into a meaningful reaction which can be recognised as no longer necessary. Freud had early in his training, when he sought help from Bernheim, come to equate the events under hypnosis which afterwards appeared to be forgotten with the traumas of neurotics, which are then forgotten and repressed from consciousness but continue to produce emotional disturbances in the form of symptoms.

The examples I have given above were produced by hypnotic commands. In this method the hypnotised person transfers the power of his superego upon the hypnotist and in a somnolent state regresses to an infantile dependency upon an omnipotent parental figure, represented by the hypnotist; he introjects his commands and they take the place of the ego functions. But when he returns to his grown-up state, to his normal conscious self, his ego once again takes over and the influence of the hypnotic suggestions tends to wane.

There is, however, another method of hypnotic induction which has found favour among hypnotists and is considered to be more effective; it is also nearer in many respects to the processes responsible for psychic and somatic disturbances. In distinction to the hypnotic phenomena produced by the 'command reaction', this method is directed to inducing imaginary situations which evoke emotional responses. One can induce all kinds of situations which evoke feelings of pleasure or danger, elation or anxiety, and it is, moreover, possible to observe in considerable detail a person's reactions to such situations. One has to bear in mind that while it is actually no more than the patient's imagination which is aroused, it feels to him to be completely real.

For instance, one can make a hypnotised person see himself self-surrounded by flowers and his sense of smell will be aroused, or if he is told to walk on a newly grown lawn, he will experience the smell of a new mown lawn, or if he sees himself walking uphill on a stony path, he will feel the strain upon his muscles and the discomfort to his feet and experience the pain of hitting some rocks which are in his way. Or he can be made to drive a car and see another car suddenly swerve into his path and a crash seems inevitable, and he will feel his heart racing or a spasm in his throat or stomach. Any situation of acute danger can be induced and the physiological responses to such situations can be observed. Indeed, the patient can be made acutely aware of his reactions and to describe them with an exactitude which is rarely possible in the normal state.

Gradually I came to recognise this capacity for increased awareness of bodily processes under hypnosis, and consider it to be of particular importance in therapy. I realised that the dramatically increased awareness of specific bodily disturbances and the patient's capacity to relate them to their emotional causes could be an important therapeutic tool. Moreover, awareness of bodily disturbances, and an insight into their emotional and psychological causes, combined with age regression, in order to trace the long forgotten origins of emotional disturbances whenever they occurred in the life of a patient would present a significant advance in analytic psychotherapy. Thus hyper-awareness of bodily disturbances together with the capacity of age regression to traumatic situations which have actually occurred in the life of the patient, often going back to infancy and childhood, became a focal point of my therapeutic method.

Hypnotic age regression, which has been known for some time and practised amongst hypnotic psychotherapists, is by itself not enough to bring about a liberation from neurotic symptoms if it is not combined with a liberation from the bodily tensions and organic contractions which both express as well as maintain the neurotic disturbances. Conversely, physical attempts to remove tensions and contractions or to discharge the pent up emotions without enabling the patient to understand their emotional causes will not in the long run remove them, for the psychic driving force behind them will continue to operate. I have found that by concentrating a person's mind upon his muscular and organic disturbances, he can be brought to understand what is causing them, what actually goes on in his mind and why he is tightening his chest, shoulders, stomach, legs, pelvis, or his jaws, or his limbs, why his chest hurts and why his heart is constricted or his breathing impaired, and comprehend their meaning as reactions to certain emotional states. I can ask a person with a paralysed arm what it is thinking and why it is paralysed or numbed. Many psychosomatic diseases originate as childhood reactions which then become frozen, so to speak, and fixated as a continuously repeated psychological pattern.

But again I must make a proviso that it is not enough to enable a patient to remember how and why his neurotic symptoms originated. One has to encourage him to fight against self-destructive and sometimes life-denying attitudes which he had without realising it adopted in his character and life style. He has to acquire a vision of new possibilities and fresh orientations towards life. But this does not mean that the therapist has to impose his ideas of health and well-being or moral attitudes upon the patient. Each individual has to discover in himself the aims and purposes which make his life worth living, but the therapist should not be indifferent to his search and to his battle to free himself from the old taboos, irrational fears, shocks and insults, his sense of isolation, rejection and worthlessness which had injured him emotionally and somatically. The patient should be encouraged to discover the pleasure of his bodily sensations and the satisfactions gained from the exercise of his innate rational capabilities. It is the aim of what we may call an affirmative therapy, not only analytic but also creative, to lead the patient to free himself from the mental as well as physical prison to which his neurosis has condemned him, and to enable him to enjoy his body and his mind in a way that he can feel to be healthy as well as gratifying.

In the following pages I shall give some examples of the methods I have adopted towards this end. It is a method which is in many ways more complex and varied than traditional forms of psychoanalysis and its derivatives. We may call it multidimensional, and it needs considerable concentration on the part of the therapist, quickness of mind, responsiveness and empathy, but above all a sense of respect for what is healthy in his patient and what he is capable of. It also requires a proper theoretical understanding of the development and transformations of the libido and the fundamental concepts of psychoanalysis. I shall therefore devote the next chapter to an overview of the early development of the individual, with particular reference to the somatic dimension of psychological processes.

5 How We Become What We Are

1. THE INTERNAL OBJECT

One is bound to ask why the emotional conflicts which have their origins in infancy and childhood continue to dominate the psyche of adults. One can speak of unconscious memories which influence a person's mind, and while this is quite correct it still does not explain why the dramas, traumas, fears and rages of the small child play such a dominant role in the formation of a person's character and of his neurotic symptoms. However, we are able to explain this phenomenon if we consider the process of introjection, whereby the primary objects of the child's libido are internalised and exercise their influence as an internal presence. Freud has called the internalised object the superego, but he was mostly concerned with the father-figure, whose internal presence operates as a protective as well as punishing authority, as a model for the boy's masculine identity and, at the same time, as a source of anxiety and guilt feelings; the boy both loves and hates his father, he depends upon him and wants to be rid of him, and this ambiguity culminates in the Oedipus complex, with its fateful consequences for the psychic life of individuals as well as of cultures.

Melanie Klein, however, has drawn attention to the intense interaction between the child and its mother, and related the process of introjection to the infant's experience of the mother's fulfilling or rejective attitudes. She stressed the primacy of the maternal superego and its importance in the psychic life of individuals. It is now recognised that the internal object exists on all levels of the libido, and plays an important role during the various stages of our development, long before the emergence of the superego and the Oedipus complex in the Freudian sense. This variant of the Freudian concept enables us to penetrate to the deeper and earlier levels of a person's psychic processes and his conflicts.

However, while the process of introjection is generally accepted and its meaning as a psychoanalytic term taken for granted, it is not sufficiently recognised that introjection first of all, and most fundamentally, operates on the somatic level, when the infant experiences the mother's feelings and attitudes and re-enacts them with its own body. Only gradually is her somatic presence transferred to the psychic system, where she becomes a mental presence within the child's ego.

Indeed, the process of introjection occurs with greatest intensity during the earliest periods of a person's life. We can say that the infant takes in the mother's libido from her breast, and recognises it as an internal, physical experience; it incorporates not only the milk from the mother but the libido that comes from her breast and from her whole being. Melanie Klein has frequently pointed to the fact that it is not only the nourishment, the milk, which is all-important. It is the child's sensation of her libido, her feelings of pleasure and joyfulness, or her state of anxiety and, indeed, the whole state of mind which the child incorporates and becomes aware of as an internal experience.

It is one of the extraordinary discoveries of depth analysis that the infant is intensely aware of its mother's feelings and attitudes towards it, how she loves her child, desires or resents it, whether she feels pleased or anxious, generous with her pleasure feelings or reserved, doubtful, rejective, unsure or insecure. It is difficult for a grown-up person to comprehend the symbiotic interaction between mother and child, unless we bear in mind that its sensation of the mother is all there is for the child in its struggle for survival in an unknown world. It has not yet acquired a sense of proportion, which comes from an awareness of past and present, and of a capacity to judge the quality of an experience in relationship to those it has experienced before. The moment is eternity for the infant and its very life depends upon what is happening to it at any given instant. All it has is a need for love and good sensations, and if these are not present it panics. What we may call fear or disappointment is for the infant all-pervading terror.

It can be said that at first the infant is not aware of a world which is separate or outside itself, and its experiences of the mother are confined to its own sensations. Thus incorporation fundamentally means taking into itself the mother's sensations and attitudes, and the child re-enacts them with its own body; it is through its physiological responses that the child experiences the mother.

But of course the child's responses to the primary object take place via the sense organs, which at first are fairly undifferentiated and could be called polymorphous or holistic, a kind of telepathic empathy. As the sensory receptors are not yet connected to the prefrontal lobes of the cortex, the infant does not perceive objects but experiences sensations, which in turn evoke emotions. But the child's unspecified sensations pick up the mother's own polymorphous feelings – of which she may be quite unconscious – and introjects them so that they are experienced as its own.

It is perhaps difficult to put these things into words, for the infant's psyche or rather, its organismic responses operate in a manner which does not know language, and before it has acquired an ego, while we attempt to describe these processes via our own ego system and by using words. However, there is no doubt that the emotional interactions between the baby and its mother are very powerful indeed, even while its mind is not developed sufficiently to have a sense of self and to perceive objects.

While the infant's experiences of its environment are largely unspecified and have not reached the stage of perception, all its senses are fully operative, and the most important among them are the mouth and the lips, for they are the primary areas of contact with a life-providing object. Indeed, the lips are quite extraordinarily sensitive, they are the focus of the child's libido, and we might say that it feels and knows with its lips, that its whole information and orientation system is centred upon them. Connected with the sensations of the lips and mouth is the sensation of taste. Again we have to adjust our grown-up concept of taste in order to understand the infant, for it not only tastes the physical sensations of the nipple and the milk but above all the quality of its mother's libido and her often unconscious attitudes towards the child. Her feelings of pleasure and joy will make her nipple and her milk taste sweet and pleasant, while anxious or rejective attitudes will produce in the child a sour or bitter or unpleasant taste. This taste experience will in turn produce expansive, joyful, and trustful, or frightened, contractive and rejective reactions. Sour taste evokes tension and tightness in the lips, whereas a sweet taste will produce expansive reactions in the musculature, as in a smile, which we can recognise as an expression of pleasure.

These primary responses involve the whole incorporative system and spread from the lips to the mouth, to the jaws, the throat, the oesophagus, the solar plexus and the stomach. For, after all, these are the channels by which the life-providing processes take place, and it is particularly the stomach which receives the nourishment and its libido, and it will replicate the sensations of the lips as well as their physiological responses. Sour and repulsive sensations in the lips produce sour, repulsive and anxious sensations in the stomach. We can say that the lips, which for the infant are the first to establish contact with the world outside, evaluate with their sense of taste its life outside the womb and act as a signalling system to which all the incorporative activities respond. The way the world tastes indicates whether it loves the child, whether the child is accepted and loved, and whether it can love itself. Mother's good feeling makes the child feel good, expansive and accepted, and the stomach will enact those feelings. If the world – primarily represented by the mother – feels good and tastes good, then the baby itself feels good, and if the world feels bad, baby feels bad. Let me reiterate the basic principle that if the mother withdraws her libido, then the baby's libido withdraws, and with it the organic function associated with the intake process pulls back, withdraws and tightens up. But these responses evoke fear and will manifest themselves in rage, choking, breathlessness, rigidities of the peripheral and back muscles, outbursts of aggression, tantrums, and what would later be called epileptic fits. Aggression and rage is a response of the organism to the withdrawal of libido that is experienced as a barrier to gratification, which the infant has to penetrate, in order to make contact with the feelings of life, which have disappeared or have remained hidden. Biting, screaming and kicking as well as an increase in blood pressure are mechanisms of aggression designed to release the organism from its tension and to counteract the withdrawal reflex. We can say that primary aggression in its many manifestations is a way of getting access to libidinous responses, a signalling system indicating the infant's needs, as well as a release from its blocks and tensions, and to gain access to the libido that has been denied.

2. PRIMARY RESPONSES AND CHARACTER FORMATION

Unless these expressions of the infant's fears and aggressiveness gain the appropriate response from the parents in terms of reassurance and warmth, they are likely to become fixated and lay the foundations to the individual's future physiological structure and his reflexes and, eventually, for his psychological characteristics. We might say that what we are, what sort of individual we develop into, is largely determined by the physiological-emotional responses which we come to adopt in early childhood. These responses are almost too manifold to describe, but we can include facial expressions, the musculature of the lips, the jaws, the anticipatory attitudes of the forehead, the chin, the structure of the throat and neck musculature, the thorax, the posture of shoulders and chest, the solar plexus, the stomach, the pelvis, the thighs and even the feet. We can make a large generalisation and categorise these reflexes into expansion or contraction, and the almost endless variety of interactions between them and the manifold characters they produce make up the variety of human personalities.

The solar plexus in particular plays an important role in the incorporative process. It can be considered as a primitive brain which evaluates and judges whether the object which the mouth wants to take in and swallow is acceptable and satisfying, or whether it is dangerous or hostile. If the taste of an object or its visual appearance indicates that it is not acceptable, then the solar plexus constricts and attempts to prevent its entry into the stomach. Even if such an object is swallowed, the solar plexus signals danger and will reject it – it will cause a sense of revulsion and attempt to regurgitate it. If animals, and this includes human beings, cannot rid themselves of this object, the sense of revulsion remains, the solar plexus will continue to feel anxious and constricted and the stomach will remain unfulfilled. While animals will have no difficulty in actually vomiting out unwanted food that has been swallowed, grown-ups humans, unable to rid themselves of unwanted objects or the unwanted feelings of objects, will experience painful tensions in the solar plexus, nausea and a general feeling of unease. Such people will feel constantly hungry and become habituated to stuffing themselves, and will only desist if they feel that the stomach is full to bursting and cannot take any more. But even then the hunger remains and with it a sense of discontent. In some individuals compulsive stuffing will often be associated with bulimia, when, however much they put into their stomach, the solar plexus signals that what they have pushed down is unacceptable and they are overtaken by a sense of revulsion which leads to vomiting.

I had a patient who as a child used to eat everything she could get hold of and became very fat. She hated herself, and her self-hatred expressed her hatred towards the introjected object, the alien, sadistic and hostile mother upon whom she nevertheless depended. She wanted to reject her mother, as she felt rejected by her, but as she could not live without her, her rejective hatred was a source of acute anxiety and had to be repressed. She had to restore her mother's presence, becoming over-dependent upon her; she had to internalise and identify with her and at the same time wanted to deny the internal mother and herself in a syndrome of self-hatred and self-denial. She could not accept herself – she felt unreal, as if she did not really exist. Under hypnosis she became aware of an acute peripheral insensitivity, an inability to feel herself, and of a tight knot in her solar plexus, and she realised that she always felt empty and in a state of 'raging hunger'. She experienced an intense conflict in her lips, which on the one hand were tight and tense in a rejective state, and on the other hand yearned for warmth and contact. But whenever she reached out for love or acceptance, she felt a nasty taste in her, a feeling that the world would reject her and that she was unacceptable.

Besides the fundamental signalling system of taste transmitted by the lips, all the other senses operate in the process of our physiological responses. Taste connects, interacts with a sense of vision, smell, hearing and touch. In other words, we take into ourselves the world around us (not merely receive passively, but actively reach out and incorporate) with all our senses. The visual sense is activated from the second or third day, but the baby does not see as we can see; as its cortical system is not yet connected with the visual sense, it is not able to recognise the specific configuration and meaning of objects. However, while the infant does not perceive the objects around it, it will receive sensations which emanate from them. It will react strongly to pleasant or unpleasant colours or shapes, and experience them in its body. Light colours, without being too glaring, will produce expansive, pleasurable feelings, as will harmonious, soft shapes, while sudden, sharp movements, represented by sharp, edgy shapes, will produce anxiety and often panic. As grown-ups we still look for warm, harmonious patterns which we find pleasurable and reassuring in landscape and architecture, while paintings quite clearly symbolise certain emotional meanings by their colours and configurations. Just think of the contrast between a Raphael and a Francis Bacon, quite apart from the actual content of the picture. We seek an environment, landscape or urban architecture which is relaxing, expansive, accepting and assuring, and want to escape from the disharmonies, and sharp, harassing and grey, colourless world that surrounds us in many areas.

The so-called magic of touch: again the contrast between the aggressive or mean or tight and loveless touch, as against the warm and loving contact with another living being. We speak of green fingers, and it seems that even vegetables and flowers respond to a loving hand that handles them, and of course all animals seek body contact and a caressing touch, and animal lovers are well aware of this. As for the sense of sound, it is interesting to note that when I regressed some patients to the embryonic state after the seventh month, the most pronounced sensations they reported were the sounds of the mother's heartbeat and the symphonic cacophony of her digestive tract and breathing.

What was even more startling was the embryo's acute response to the mother's state of anxiety, manifested in the irregularity of her breathing and her heartbeat. The impact of sound upon our emotions is of course well known, and music as well as singing represent to us the whole range of emotions which we can experience. Farmers speak to their animals, and it seems to be true that cows yield more milk if they are made to feel good with pleasant music or singing. It is also true that there is music in all of us, even though the form of music which we harbour in our souls and which we seek out varies considerably. One speaks of these things as God-given or, in more fashionable terms, as being genetically inherited. However, even as God claims to have given us a measure of free will, and cannot be held responsible for every nastiness or stupidity perpetrated by his human creations, so genetic programming allows for a wide range of variability in the human personality. The more one investigates the psychological factor, the more one has to recognise its impact upon the development of a person's character.

While I have mentioned the positive response to warm and harmonious visual as well as sound and touch sensations, it is nevertheless true to say that many people are drawn towards aggressive, jagged, dark images and seem to enjoy them, in architecture as well as in paintings. Who can doubt that much of what goes for music in our time is aggressive and brutal, jagged and disharmonious, and increasingly accompanied by a kind of dancing which is jerky, aggressive, sudden in its movement and seems to defy all notion of harmony, softness and beauty? Indeed, we find that much of musical entertainment is associated with violent bodily movement ('power dancing' and 'spastic dancing'), which reminds one of infantilistic expressions of anger, defiance and outrage. Acting out tantrums and spasms seems to be a favourite musical art form which expresses popular feelings in a de-sublimated expression, of which I have spoken as characteristic of small children.

Let me reiterate that on the deepest, infantile and

unconscious level, the individual derives his identity from the primary object whose libido he incorporates and feels inside himself. We have seen that pleasurable sucking, the sensations of the libido of the breast and the milk will provide a sense of gratification in the child which feels the good object inside itself and will feel good. The sensation of the bad libido emanating from the mother will arouse aggressive forms of incorporation. Aggression towards the object becomes, through the process of internalisation, aggression against the self. While the satisfying experience of aggression towards an object is a basis of sadism, aggression towards the internalised object turns sadism into masochism. This not only produces a wide range of paranoias, anxieties and forms of self-hatred as well as inadequacy feelings, but also many physiological disturbances and tensions, which one could call forms of auto-aggression. One does to the internal object – the self – what one wants to do to the external object, which one has introjected. Individuals like this will experience painful cramps in solar plexus and stomach whenever they are angry, whenever they encounter situations they 'cannot stomach', cannot accept, and will attack the internal bad object. The early responses of the infant tend to become structured into reflexes, and largely determine a person's subsequent physical as well as psychological characteristics.

3. DEVELOPMENT AND TRANSFORMATIONS OF THE LIBIDO

A person's character development is not merely a matter of the contingencies and accidents of his environmental conditions. There is a certain innate direction in every person's psychobiological evolution, which Freud called the development and transformations of the libido. He found that the libido undergoes a number of transformations in the course of a person's development from infancy to adulthood, and that, furthermore, these transformations occur with considerable regularity in all individuals. The regularity of libidinous transformations emboldened Freud to formulate a law of sexual development which has since found ample confirmation in the psychoanalysis of children and adults. However, he also discovered that a person's development can be arrested at a certain stage of his evolution, and that his development may be blocked and produce a wide range of neurotic conflicts.

It is one of the corner-stones of psychoanalytic theory that the sexual drive, or libido, is not confined to genital sexuality, that children are not sexless, as had been assumed, but that there exists in the child a wide spectrum of sexual drives and that at certain periods of his development certain drives become dominant, i.e. attain primacy over others. While the sexual drive exists from the very beginning of a person's life, it is connected to a wide range of vital functions and has to pass through a complicated process before it attains the characteristics of what we call the normal genital sexuality of adults. Sexuality thus is not an instinct that manifests itself in a particular form only but is more like an energy that undergoes many transformations in an individual's life.

In my book *The Unknown Self* I deal with the development of the libido in the individual, its disturbances and conflicts, and it forms the background to my therapeutic method: 'In the development of individuals, in the unfolding of their organic and psychic potential, the libido attaches itself to a succession of activities, and at various stages gives them primacy over the others. By means of the libidinous urges the individual is compelled to follow the needs of the organism. It is as if nature had provided a pleasure-seeking energy that attaches itself to the important self-preserving and species-preserving activities, and motivates these activities by an almost irresistible drive, which, if fulfilled, rewards the organism with a sense of pleasure, while frustration or denial arouses sensations of anxiety, aggressiveness and tension.

'While the species-preserving functions of the individual

in the form of genital sexuality are given high emphasis by nature, it is necessary for the individual, as a link in the chain of the life of a species, to preserve itself and to develop its potentials, and for that purpose the self-preserving functions and those directed to the growth and the development of the individual organism are cathexed with sufficient quanta of libido to ensure that they are carried out. In the development of the individual, in the process of its evolution and growth, libidinous energy is channelled to a succession of vitally necessary functions. We can define the development of the pregenital libido as serving the purpose of:

1) directing the child towards oral activities for the incorporation of food and communion with mother;

2) establishing the child's awareness of itself as a separate and distinct individual by making the self an object of libidinous gratification. We call this primacy narcissism, and it is the foundation for the development of the ego and a sense of self;

3) establishing the process of self-projection, which is motivated by the anal libido, assuring the child of its sense of identity in the world and its capacity of producing and manipulating objects.'

We might say that the early primacies of the libido serve the preservation and development of the individual, and at the conclusion of the development devoted to individual self-preservation there occurs a concentration of libido upon the genitals. Of course the pregenital or infantile primacies of the libido do not cease to operate with the advent of sexual maturity, nor is the genital libido absent in infancy. At certain stages of his development the individual is dominated by a libidinous primacy, but the so-called normal person is able to develop further, and in some measure enter the next stage on the scale of his personal evolution. In the neurotic personality' the degree of fixation is more pronounced and will continue to dominate him. He remains stuck, so to speak, in a halfway house on the road of his psychic development and will face the world with the expectations and desires of his infantile primacies, and the development of his ego will be impaired. The so-called normal person's character will also be influenced by certain primacies, but he will be able to sublimate and accommodate them to the needs of reality, a process which is the chief task of the ego. As can be seen, I am employing here an evolutionary model in the aetiology of neurosis as well as of character. Neither character nor neurotic symptoms should be taken as fixed phenomena, either genetically determined or divinely ordained and classified as static entities. In keeping with the classic psychoanalytic model, I am concerned with their history.

While I have drawn attention to the infant's primary physiological responses in the process of internalisation, it is not long before the mind is activated and physiological processes are expressed in psychological terms. The physiological processes continue to operate but they are picked up by the mind and transformed into psychological activity. And by psychological, we mean thoughts, images, fantasies, apprehension, fear, horror, pleasure, desire, sense of isolation, or confidence and security.

As the sensorium is gradually connected with the cortical and prefrontal functions, sensations become perceptions, reflexes are largely transformed into volition, and the mind creates a new territory of experience, the sense of self begins to develop and with it the ego functions begin to develop.

4. THE DOMINANT ROLE OF THE VISUAL SENSE

We must remember that in humans it is the visual cortex which is the most highly developed part of the cortical functions and acquires a dominant role. Our perceptions, or we may say, how we present our sensations and emotions to our minds, occur largely in the form of visual images, and not only perceptions of the world outside us, but our feelings, fears, as well as ideas have their representation in visual images. The internalised object is thus represented in images expressing the conflicts and ambiguities of the child's earliest experiences. For instance, a tight and negative mother figure which has produced fear and aggression in the child is reproduced as a frightening and aggressive image, a witch with threatening teeth or fangs or claws and an angry look which continues to frighten the child and is retained in the unconscious mind of grown-ups, producing states of anxiety for which there seems to be no apparent reason. It is therefore not merely a realistic image of the mother or of the father or, later, other objects of the libido which are reproduced in the imagery of the individual. Thus we can say that the feelings of rage or love, of pleasure and confidence or distaste and insecurity, which have been aroused by the primary contacts and continue to dominate the mind, are projected upon the primary objects and as such presented in visual terms. Neurotics, as well as what we call ordinary sane persons who have had frightening and aggressive experiences in their early childhood, will harbour images of monsters and ghouls, spiky, clawing and generally frightening pictures which dominate their psyche. As we grow up we manage to repress these images from consciousness, and the ego will learn to master them (more or less), whereas neurotics, whose ego functions are weak, can feel threatened by such images, whilst in psychotics such images swamp the mind and are perceived as real. It is quite normal for children to play act monsters as a kind of catharsis, and indeed they appear in our dreams and in popular entertainments when we relish being frightened by them. However, we normally are not conscious of them as part of ourselves. To give an example:

An amateur actress, aged 32, who also worked in a theatrical agency, suffered from acute shyness in her personal relationships as well as at work, paranoid anxieties and a sense of isolation. However, on the stage she was expansive, highly talented and exuberant. She had become a compulsive eater and had put on a lot of weight which increased her feelings of being unattractive and unwanted. We analysed many aspects of her childhood and youth but could not break through her defensive withdrawal symptoms, paranoid anxieties and stuffing compulsions. I decided to hypnotise her and under hypnosis asked her to see herself as she really wanted to be. She saw herself as a beautiful, stimulating woman, confidently assertive and somewhat challenging in her attitudes to men. She observed, however, that this person, although very confident and attractive, showed signs that she had suffered pains and had known tragedies. I then asked her to get this lady to take her back to situations which were painful and tragic and to observe what was happening. She then saw herself very frightened and rigid with anxiety, and when I asked her to look at what it was that frightened her, she saw an angry and vicious bull, with large, threatening horns, his nostrils flaring and his teeth expressing ferocious rage. He came towards her, and she became terrified and begged me to let her get out of this situation. I calmly and kindly reassured her that she would be all right, that I am with her and she should have a good look at the bull and find out what he represents. She straightaway said that it was her father, and began to cry. He was very angry and she loved him, and she was very upset for him and she also felt his rage.

I then asked her to investigate why he was so angry and what pain he suffered from. The patient then saw herself as a girl of about five years old, standing there very rigidly in almost complete darkness, completely alone and frightened. I then asked her to look around to see where she was, but she could not see anything in the darkness and felt completely alone and isolated: in fact, she did not feel that she existed at all. We can say that she was in a state of incipient catatonia, a sense of isolation and absence of self feeling which continued in later life, although her ego was able to repress it sufficiently to prevent it from developing into catatonia. It was obvious that she could not deal with her father's distress and give him the love and reassurance which she wanted to give, because she did not receive enough libidinous contact from her mother. I asked her to look for her mother. After a short while her mother appeared. Again she began to cry and saw her mother as a distant figure who would not relate to the patient or give her much recognition. I asked her to go up to her mother and embrace her. The mother responded, but she did so out of a sense of obligation, and her embrace was devoid of warmth and felt artificial. I then asked the girl to go out into the garden, which was sunny and warm and full of flowers, and to skip and dance and enjoy herself. After a while she responded and started to dance, and she saw the flowers looking at her, and she cried a little but felt better. When she woke up she could feel her body and it had a feeling of lightness and mobility. But she felt shaken in her mind and confused, and said that there were some important things going on which would take a little while to absorb. She also realised that her stomach was always empty and pervaded by an unpleasant feeling. In subsequent sessions I brought her back to infancy, when she saw images of witches with grimacing and angry faces, frightening teeth and claws threatening to attack the girl and at the same time keeping her at bay. We eventually analysed the mother's emotional disturbances and the reasons for her hostility to her daughter as well as her husband.

As a girl this patient loved her father and wanted to give him the love and reassurance which her mother could not give him. The girl wanted to make him happy but felt inadequate to do this because she lacked the confidence of her own libido. She would enact a confident and warm person on the stage, able to make everybody laugh and feel good, but in her personal life she felt a failure like her father. She did not realise that she caused people to behave in a rejective manner, because she acted with fear and mistrust towards them.

In our observations of the processes of introjection and

the sense organs involved we must not omit to mention the genitals, for they are from a very early age centres of libidinous activity and among the most sensitive and responsive areas of our body. Even in infancy the sensations of the mother's libido are registered in the genitals, and the child's sense of pleasure will evoke expansive reactions, whereas unpleasure or anxiety will evoke anxious and constrictive responses. It is well known that baby boys will have erections upon the experience of pleasure sensations and no doubt girls' vaginal sensations are equally aroused. We can go further and say that as the mother's vaginal feelings are stimulated by the pleasure of breast feeding, the child picks up these sensations and experiences them in its genitals. An anxious or angry mother will evoke anxious sensations in the child's genitals. When the child reaches the period of the first puberty at about the age of four or five and the genitals acquire the libidinous primacy, these will be particularly sensitive to its parents' genital characteristics. Every girl will show curiosity towards her father and want to explore the state and nature of his sexuality, and in her encounters will become acutely aware of his attitudes and responses towards her sexual explorations. She wants not only to explore him but also to show herself to him and test his responses to her. If he responds without fear and shows pleasure it will register in her genitals with confidence in her pleasure sensations and she will, so to speak, introject his sensations with her vagina, the vagina will re-enact his genital characteristics. This does not mean that the father should react to his daughter's overt or hidden sexual advances with his own sexual desire but with appreciation, acknowledgement and without fear. Indeed, it is one of the problems in father-daughter relationships that the father who is not confident or secure in his sexuality will be afraid of being aroused by her and meet her investigations with rejection. Conversely, he will in some cases impose his own sexual demands upon her and frighten her. These interactions equally apply to the mother-son relationship. The boy will also sense the mother's responses to his desires and re-enact them. These early forms of genital identification tend to play a decisive role in the sexual development of individuals.

For instance: a young woman who suffered from retentive syndromes and loss of menstruation also experienced vaginal anxieties and anaesthesia. Her pelvis was chronically pulled back, her shoulders hunched and tense, and she had a history of arthritic symptoms in her hands and fingers. She was very insecure about her sexuality, found it difficult to trust men and generally took a deprecating attitude towards her own sexual feelings. Her mother was a forbidding and discontented person, and as a girl she turned to her father for reassurance and love. She remembered, however, that on many occasions when she wanted to be close to him and to embrace him and feel the closeness of his body to her that he withdrew and pulled himself back so as to avoid any possible intimate contact. She eventually re-enacted his withdrawal movements and the anxiety which he felt became a dominant factor in her own attitudes towards sexual feelings. Indeed, she became somewhat paranoic about men and had to repress her own genital arousal and erotic contact. She had repressed these encounters with her father from her memory and was not aware of her emotional or physical attitudes which had become uncontrolled reflexes.

It has been said that the unconscious is our fate, inasmuch as it determines the roles which we adopt in our relationships. No doubt we re-enact our childhood images in our grown-up existence, and tend to perpetuate our earliest relationships with our parents and siblings. It is thus the unconscious psyche which is the manager of our reality. This does not mean that we can ignore the social reality into which we have been propelled, but the way we respond to it, perceive it, master and are able to change it, is the concern of depth psychological investigation and therapy.

6 First Encounters

1. HOW TO COMMUNICATE WITH PATIENTS

A neurologist of my acquaintance asked me to see a young man whom he considered to be a congenital idiot with an IQ of 60 – 70 and severely depressive. He thought there might possibly be a connection between this patient's depression and his intellectual retardation, and knowing about my interest in such cases, he asked me to investigate. I agreed, and a week later this young man appeared in my office. 'Appeared' is rather an apt way of describing this, as he did not say anything but just stood there with his head bowed down, looking at his feet. I asked him some preliminary questions confirming his name, address, age and what he thought was the matter with him. I tried to engage him in some light conversation, but he just uttered some grunting noises in response, incapable of any communication. There was something about his demeanour which indicated a sense of tragedy and despair as well as an overwhelming sulkiness. He defied my approaches not with anger but with a kind of fear. He seemed to be hiding himself as if he wanted to disappear. I urged him to look at me, and when he did so I had the distinct feeling that he wanted to tell me something but could not do so; but above all I had the surprising impression of a bright and intelligent person badly frightened.

I tried for half an hour to get some conversation going but it was quite impossible to get any response or any sense out of him, and I began to get depressed myself. It would have been easy to write him off as severely mentally deficient, a diagnosis which would be made easy in face of his IQ, but I was not satisfied with this. So I told him that I would hypnotise him to find out what was going on in his unconscious mind. He seemed quite happy about this and appeared to welcome my suggestion. I used hypnosis without any trouble, and rather than asking him questions I told him to walk about the room. He did so with his head down as before. Then I asked him to raise his head and look in front of him. He tried to do so, but after a few seconds he lowered his head again. It became obvious that he had great difficulty in following my instruction, and trying to do so produced considerable anxiety. I instructed him firmly to raise his head, to stand up straight and look in front. He tried very hard this time, but as he raised his head he began to shake and perspire and to be overwhelmed by an anxiety which amounted to a state of panic. I told him that he was obviously frightened but that he must look in front and observe carefully what he saw that made him frightened and to tell me whatever he saw. Eventually, after much trepidation, he looked steadfastly, and he saw his father with his face distorted in rage and shouting at him, saying that he was useless, incapable and a source of great disappointment, a useless and lazy good-for-nothing. Indeed, he told his son that he was deeply ashamed of him. At first the patient was overtaken by acute spasms of shaking. He began to cry. Then I noticed rage and that his shaking was not merely an expression of fear and horror but also a sense of outrage.

After a while he became fairly relaxed, and I let him sit down and sleep. When he woke up his eyes were much clearer than before, and he looked at me with an expression of amazement and an intimation of gratitude. In subsequent sessions we repeated the experience, and eventually he told me a tragic story of an ambitious and impatient father, and we were able to analyse the father's psychological problems. Eventually his IQ improved significantly, and he is now a mechanic like his father and is running his own garage.

I mention this case because it illustrates a first encounter which presented all the signs of an insuperable barrier to communication and appeared to make any psychotherapy impossible. However, his inability to communicate provided an important key to the understanding of his intellectual and emotional disturbance.

Another case, entirely different, indeed, the very opposite: I had treated a patient who suffered from anxiety states and whose wife refused any physical contact with him. As this patient got better, it seemed obvious that it would not be possible for him to get well while his wife, whom he loved, continued to rebuff him in a violent and aggressive manner, as she had done for a number of years. From his description it was obvious that she was a very disturbed person with many signs of psychosis. She had psychoanalytic treatment for three years four times a week, without any sign of improvement. As her husband was quite understandably distressed, I suggested that he contact her analyst; the analyst rejected his complaints rather brusquely and even intimated that he must himself be neurotically disturbed for interfering with her treatment, obviously not wanting his wife to get better. He begged me to see his wife for he was afraid that she might suffer some injury, for every time she left her analyst's house she drove about London in her car in a state of disorientation and hysteria. I was reluctant to see her, not wanting to breach professional etiquette, but in the end I thought to hell with etiquette and agreed to see her. Much to my surprise, having had a mental picture of a tough, aggressive virago of a woman, a very attractive and lively person entered my consulting room. Instead of asking her to lie on a couch and start free association, I spoke to her as if I had known her for a long time (as indeed I had, even while my impressions of her were coloured by her husband's tales of agony, having had to suffer his wife's implacable rejection). And, indeed, she had known me for some time, having heard of me from her husband. So I talked to her in a friendly and open manner to make her feel at ease, and after a while she exclaimed with surprise: 'George, you are talking to me, my psychoanalyst never really talked to me'. She told me that in most of her sessions she felt utterly alone without any contact with the analyst, who would remain silent hour after hour and only occasionally make some interpretation which the patient would not understand, only exacerbating her sense of isolation. I told her that this is an orthodox practice, and I explained shortly the theory behind it, its advantages and possible dangers, and why I no longer adopt it. As I talked to her about my own beliefs and attitudes, she seemed to gain more confidence in herself, and showed pleasure that I confided in her and found her important and intelligent enough as a person to understand my thoughts. After a while, I happened to make some jokes and we laughed heartily. She was utterly amazed and exclaimed: 'George, you are laughing with me'. She found this an utterly new experience and quite obviously exhilarating. The point is that hardly anybody ever laughed with her. She soon came to accept me as a friend, and would talk intimately and with considerable freedom.

These two patients represented quite different, indeed, opposite forms of a first encounter. While with one I could not find a way of communicating at all at first and had to adopt an hypnotic method in order to penetrate his profound resistances, the other was only too willing to talk to me but needed the assurance and, as it were, the example of my conversation in order to release her from her defences.

One of the decisions which one has to make during the early stages of therapy concerns the depth of treatment one intends to pursue. There are cases when depth therapy is either unnecessary or counter-productive. One of the most 'successful cures' I have achieved was with a young man who came to me because he was impotent with his girlfriend. He was a well-built, healthy fellow of twenty-two who was deeply distressed at his failure. He had known this girl for about four weeks and felt obliged to have sex with her in order to fulfil what he thought were her expectations and also the pressures of what he called modern sexual morality, but he actually resented this pressure upon him. Indeed, he gave himself no chance to find out whether he desired her or not. I spent an hour with him explaining his conflict and advised him to let himself feel whether he wanted her or not and make his decision entirely according to his own feelings. He arrived at the next appointment waving the money for the consultation at me and with an expression of great satisfaction declared that he was now completely cured and was no longer in any doubt about his potency. He sent me a Christmas card about a half a year later confirming that all is well.

There are many cases when a good talk can eliminate a sense of failure and anxiety without having to have recourse to deep analysis. Indeed, prolonged analysis would only reaffirm the patient's sense of failure and helplessness.

There has been much argument whether it is the chief task of psychoanalysis to centre its attention on the patient's symptoms or on his whole personality. The chief protagonists of the 'whole person' school were Adler, Fromm and Reich, whereas Freud and his orthodox followers felt that their chief concern was to deal with the symptoms and their aetiology. The 'whole person' advocates maintain that to study symptoms without relating them to a person's character is to neglect the most important determinants of neurotic manifestations, for the form which a symptom takes is inevitably related to a person's character. I consider both attitudes, symptom-directed as well as personality-directed, to be valid as there is no need to adopt an either/or attitude.

One can say that every neurosis is a manifestation of a certain libidinous fixation, an arrest upon a certain stage of a person's development; but it is also true that every 'normal' person's character is in many respects determined by certain fixations which dominate his attitudes, desires and judgements. For instance, individuals dominated by an oral-aggressive primacy will show character traits such as greed, impatience, determination or ruthlessness, or sadism, masochism and manic-depressive dispositions.

2. CHOICE OF TREATMENT

The first task of the therapist therefore in his encounter with his patient is to define how deep his disturbance is, to what evolutionary scale of his development his fixations belong and how profound therefore his neurosis. A patient may see us, for instance, for a state of anxiety or depression, which turns out to be caused by an existential problem. Shocks or disappointments tend to weaken and even paralyse the ego, causing it to regress to earlier stages of psychological development and bring to the fore deep-seated unconscious conflicts. It is, however, often possible to ease a patient's anxiety or depression by clarifying the existential crisis which confronts him, and to strengthen his ego by helping him to find a way of dealing with it. I always make it clear to a patient that to be miserable or unhappy does not mean the same as depression, and that even a reactive state of depression does not have to be neurotic and can be counteracted by means of some appropriate action. If, however, he feels helpless and paralysed by fear, unable either to think or to act in an appropriate manner, then we must assume that his ego functions have been severely weakened and his personality has become dominated by infantile complexes and fixations. But even then we still have to assess how far he had previously proceeded on the path to maturity and whether he can be lured out of his infantile fixations and encouraged to adopt mature attitudes.

I had a patient who was a concert pianist but had become overwhelmed by panic states during performances and had to stop her career. Neurotic self-doubts and depression were the consequence of her sense of utter failure. After a few sessions, we were able to direct her attention to sexual components of her playing to an audience, to the excitement of the music and of the exhibitionistic pleasures involved. She was able to recognise and accept this, and gradually became aware that in fact she had fantasies of raising her skirt while playing and showing her legs to the audience. In fact she was a tall and beautiful woman with very libidinous legs. The fantasies had threatened to become irresistible and produced the panic attacks which forced her to end her career. She recognised the erotic force associated with her performances, and she could look me in the face while she spoke of these fantasies and frequently burst out laughing. I had become an understanding and tolerant superego and vanquished the fearsome and punishing mother-figure. Her playing improved, and she could once again give performances. However, she still felt troubled occasionally and unsure in her relationships, her shyness still had not quite disappeared, and despite her pleasure in having re-established her career, she still had feelings of inferiority. In fact we had to face infantile conflicts, some unresolved fixations upon her infantile libido, and had to go deeper into the recesses of her unconscious mind. Her main symptoms were resolved, but the deeper conflicts of her character still had to be confronted.

There are almost endless variations of this theme, impossible to present in their fullness. But for the purpose of this presentation of my therapeutic methods, I would say that if during the early sessions the patient presents his communication in a circular manner and one feels that he (or she) does not gain any new insights, when his defences provide an insuperable obstacle to self-discovery, one has to employ depth therapy. If one looks at the eyes of patients of this kind, one notices that they don't seem to be looking at what they are saying. The eyes are directed away from their communication, and one can be fairly sure that their preconscious mind is occupied with something different. Or even if they are speaking apparently openly and are prepared to discuss previously repressed desires or memories, their movements and expression do not reflect feelings connected with their disclosures, and they are communicating in a manner as if what they are saying has nothing very much to do with them.

I want to return for a moment to the controversy among psychoanalysts amounting to a clash of opposing schools which frequently adopt dogmatic positions, concerning the overriding importance of the ego functions in the development of neurotic symptoms, as against the emphasis upon the unconscious among the more traditional exponents of psychoanalysis. It seems to me that this controversy is based upon the erroneous tendency to conceive the ego functions as being largely conscious. By upholding this rather confused conception the ego psychologists intend to free psychoanalysis from the determination of the unconscious and emphasise the patient's capacity to control his psychic process. Psychoanalysis has often been accused of looking backwards, stressing the past as an iron law which determines man's conduct. It is true that to a great extent psychoanalysis considers people as the product of their history, but that is not the same as upholding the authority of the past and thereby limiting the capacity for freedom, as Fromm has implied in his criticism of Freud. I consider these battles between opposing schools quite unnecessary and even ludicrous, for there is ego psychology as well as the psychology of the deeper levels of the mind, which often operate on the unconscious level. One can of course view a person's life and his problems from many different angles and arrive at explanations according to the point of view which one adopts. There are deep levels and surface levels of the psyche, but there is no doubt that they are interconnected and operate at the same time. The ego perceives itself in its own way and the unconscious perceives itself frequently in a quite different way. There is the grown-up form of self-perception and there is the little boy or the little girl in all of us clamouring for attention, and there is the infant in its own world of drives, of desires and fears and helplessness and panic and tantrum of which the ego knows very little.

While it is true that one has to start from the surface, so to speak, and analyse the patient's ego functions – how he sees his problems and his view of himself – before one can penetrate to the deeper levels of his psyche, we have to take into account that many of his ego functions operate on the unconscious level. What Adler has called the quest for power, the inferiority complex, the life style a person had adopted in childhood and which guides his consequent pursuits as well as his view of himself, are all on the level of ego psychology, albeit unconscious.

Other 'ego psychologists', who to a very large extent have taken their cue from Adler, often without acknowledging it, emphasise the importance of personal relationships, and by analysing them attempt to rectify their disturbances. They intend to lead the patient to a healthy sense of reality, a sense of community spirit and capacity for social relationships, discipline, sense of obligation, effort making, empathy with others, respect for moral concepts and the rational evaluation of moral concepts and a capacity for making choices. These are qualities which our culture values highly and are therefore upheld as goals to be pursued in therapy. It is evident that no therapy exists in a cultural vacuum; however, it is true to say some therapeutic schools keep ethical values in the foreground of their therapeutic goal, while others emphasise them less consciously. But it is from the viewpoint of our cultural values, whether we uphold them consciously or not, that we analyse the patient's own ego attitudes, focus his attention upon them, and help him to recognise their deficiencies. But still the fact remains that he is largely unconscious of his own ego attitudes and his view of himself, and it is the task of any therapy to facilitate his recognition of those aspects of his personality which we consider to be inadequate or pathological. While this is to some extent possible by means of discussion or by free association and interpretation, these procedures have their limitations, particularly as the unconscious ego processes and the patient's self-image, his attitudes to the world, his social and personal relationships, his projections and value concepts are largely conditioned by the urges and goals of his unconscious libido which had their origins in infancy and childhood. Indeed, we must recognise that the ego construct, conscious as well as unconscious, serves the purpose of justifying and rationalising his libidinous fixations and to give them a socially accepted form, or what he considers to be a socially justified form. Moreover, the ego's chief function consists in attempts to integrate the libidinous drives into a coherent unity which makes up his personality. No individual, however sane or well-adjusted he is considered or considers himself to be, is entirely certain how well he is managing to integrate his libidinous drives into a coherent self-image, an image of his own personality and his role in society, but one can certainly say that some manage it better than others (often at the cost of having to adopt armoured and rigid attitudes, prejudices and defensive convictions). Many however do not manage to co-ordinate their conflicting urges and fears and drives, and they will find expression in neurotic symptoms. Neurotic symptoms thus, as Freud had recognised long ago, give expression to libidinous drives which the ego is unable to sublimate and co-ordinate into the personality structure, and they remain ego-alien forces, operating against the ego, so to speak, and find their expression in symbolic forms as symptoms. The conflict between the ego and the ego-alien forces of the libido result in a constant battle which can debilitate and exhaust a person. While a large part of his energies is devoted to the repression of these ego-alien forces in order to defend himself against them, his defences are frequently breached and result in self-destructive and destructive disorders.

For instance: a young man, whose mother committed suicide when he was four years old, came to hold his father responsible for her death and was consumed with rage and hatred against him. He refused to accept his father's and his stepmother's authority, he became severely ill after his mother's death, and when he recovered treated his parents as aliens to whom he felt no sense of obligation. As, however, he continued to depend upon them, he adopted attitudes designed to placate his parents and relatives and to ingratiate himself with them, which later developed into the acquisition of a 'charming personality'. He described it as his art of 'bullshitting'. But underneath there was a morass of rage which tended to break to the surface whenever he failed to get his way and to manipulate his environment by means of his charm. But having cut off real emotional contact with his parents and later with the social world around him, he developed a fantasy world dominated by manic overcompensation of his injured and isolated narcissism and felt no obligation towards the real world which he thought to be responsible for his unhappiness. While he often managed to evoke sympathy and support in his personal relationships by means of his charm, he lacked the capacity for effort making and discipline and could not persevere in any activity, job or business without at the slightest sign of criticism erupting into rage. This of course involved the destruction of any relationship on the personal or career level. Indeed, a destructive and self-destructive drive, a ceaseless revenge against the world, which he unconsciously held responsible for his mother's death, its insults and betrayals, dominated his personality. He would accuse his friends and associates of letting him down, considered them all to be useless, 'wankers and fools', and discharged his latent rage upon them. As his rages, his manic compensation and paranoid dispositions overwhelmed his ego functions and diminished his sense of reality, he considered them to be entirely justified. I shall return to this patient again later.

7 Stages of Hypnoid Depth Analysis

1. THE PHYSIOLOGICAL ROOTS OF THE PSYCHE

There is an aspect of psychoanalysis which has been given little attention, although Freud himself was aware of it, namely, the nature of sensory deprivation in the psychoanalytic setting which has an hypnotic effect upon the patient. By depriving the patient of visual and physical contact with the analyst, by making him passive and immobile, one inhibits the natural activities of his senses which seek stimuli and responses from the world around him. His mind is required to turn inwards, and the activity of his psyche becomes the focus of his attention. One thus produces a condition where the patient's perceptual field is narrowed by directing his attention upon a single object of interest, which in psychoanalysis concerns the thoughts which occur to his mind. He is asked to focus his attention entirely upon those thoughts, and to inhibit the attention-seeking process directed to the world outside. It is well known that if a person manages to direct all his attention exclusively upon a single object, as for instance a mantra, a pendulum, a light bulb, or monotonous and repetitive sounds, or a fanatic orator, hypnotic conditions are produced. While psychoanalytic technique deliberately avoids any ritual of hypnotic induction, it nevertheless produces a semi-hypnotic state where the patient tends to become aware of normally repressed psychic processes. His normal ego defences are weakened and allow unconscious mental activities to emerge to the surface. But the drawback is that the ego tends to reassert its dominance over the psychic apparatus once material unacceptable to it emerges, and will push it back again into oblivion. Or the patient will attempt to dissociate himself emotionally, and report his associations in an impersonal manner, as if they really had nothing much to do with him. While the analysis of resistances can produce interesting psychic material, patients frequently try to reinstate their defences by means of argumentative self-justifications, or by a show of complete openness and understanding which often acts as a cover behind which they would conceal their real feelings.

It seemed to me that instead of waiting for the patient to drift into the semi-hypnotic reverie of free association, it would be better to apply a hypnotic procedure. The use of hypnosis to facilitate the patient's ability to make contact with the repressed psychic material appeared to be a logical way to therapeutic success, a more effective highway to the unconscious than free association. However, it all seemed to depend upon the efficiency of the induction method employed and the results gained in this way.

There is an almost endless literature on the subject of people's hypnotisability, often replete with statistics and analysis of the conditions required, the patient's attitudes and characteristics as well as hypnotic techniques. I have over the years adopted a method of the utmost simplicity, which practically rules out the hypnotic rituals of old. I explain to the patient that I am going to hypnotise him in order to find out what goes on below the surface, and take it for granted that he understands what I mean and that he is motivated by an interest in this process of discovery. The work under hypnosis itself is entirely psychoanalytic insofar as it is a process of discovery and not an imposition of commands and conditioning.

Even in the so-called hypnotic technique which I use, I re-establish the person-to-person contact, and avoid an authoritarian or mystical feeling. I assume that the patient understands that there is something in his mind which causes his various symptoms, and that if he can understand the deeper causes of these symptoms and the conflicts in his mind, he may be able to master these conflicts and thereby overcome his symptoms. I put this across to him in the most matter of fact manner, and I find that if one appeals to a person's intelligence and respects his dignity, he is not only prepared to co-operate but usually keen to do so.

With the aid of hypnosis we create a psychological condition which makes it possible to go to the deep layers of the mind without having to undergo the laborious journey of free association, interpretation, resistance analysis and transference analysis. We can indeed start from the deep layers. One can say that psychoanalysis is an inductive process, as it begins with the manifest symptoms and conscious experiences of the patient and gradually works its way to the depth of the mind. The method we adopt can be considered to be deductive insofar as we fairly quickly enter into the unconscious areas of the psyche, which can be considered to be the roots of the patient's disturbances, and trace their development to neurotic or psychotic symptoms. And as we have seen, the roots of a person's disturbances are his physiological reactions, the reflexes which at an early stage become fixed, structured, so to speak, and we shall endeavour to start with those physiological disturbances. We have in mind a triad: physiological tensions and conflicts − their transformations into psychological conflicts − visual representations of these conflicts. All these are unconscious by the time a patient seeks treatment. He merely suffers and is aware of the last link in a complex chain of psychosomatic developments. We shall, therefore, follow in our therapy the development of a patient's disturbances, and not merely reconstruct but enable him to re-experience, re-live the history of his disease.

If we consider that the somatic reactions which have

become structured, involuntary and beyond the person's conscious control are fundamental to his character as well as his neurotic disturbances, we have to make the investigation of these somatic processes the first step of the therapy. One can even say that psychosomatic depth therapy is a kind of behavioural therapy, if one equates somatic processes with behaviour. However, this would not be correct, for the term behaviour relates to the manifest actions of an individual in response to certain environmental conditions, whereas somatic-bodily processes, even though they can be considered activities of the body, are not necessarily manifest, indeed, they take place below the threshold of perceptual awareness. He is not only unaware of internal physiological dysfunctions but also of manifest reflexes, such as hunched shoulders, pulled in chest, tightness of the abdomen, of the buttocks, rigidity of the pelvis, as well as aggressive or confused gestures with his mouth and jaws, his arms and legs. We can speak of the language of the body, or, to be more correct, we attempt to translate the emotional expressions of the body into verbal communication.

The patient may, for instance, suffer from anorexia, without being aware of his tensions in the throat and the jaws, the contractions of his solar plexus and stomach, which make it impossible to swallow food. All that is manifest is his inability to eat. But what is even less known is why the patient should suffer these contractions of his ingestive organs, what they actually mean in psychological terms and what has caused them. To make these connections, the patient has first of all to be made aware of the disturbances of his ingestive organs, and then to an understanding of their meaning and their causes. In this way the involuntary processes, the uncontrollable reflexes can gain access to the voluntary system; the ego can then re-experience the long-forgotten events which produced his physiological reactions, and learn to rearrange, so to speak, his processes of ingestion and become free from their compulsive nature. New attitudes to food and new habits of eating could thus be formed: in other words, to make the id, which has its roots in the physiological functions, accessible to the ego, to transfer the involuntary system into the voluntary system. The first part of our hypnoid analysis is therefore devoted to the awareness of the body, its neurotic malfunctions and its defence mechanisms.

2. HYPNOTIC BODY AWARENESS

The procedures of hypnoid depth analysis, which I am about to describe here, are not meant to be followed in a rigid manner, for one has to adjust the steps to be taken in this treatment to the needs and characteristics of each individual. They should be seen rather as typical or basic steps amidst a large number of possible variations.

The preliminary interview and the patient's communications of the way he perceives his problems are conducted on chairs, patient and therapist facing each other in an informal manner, sometimes drinking coffee. The hypnotic induction, on the other hand, and subsequent hypnotic analysis usually proceed with the patient reclining on the couch. We make an exception to this rule when the patient's defences feel threatened and arouse anxiety if he is made to lie in a supine position in front of the therapist. With men this can occur if they are afraid that repressed homosexual urges are aroused in this position, and in women the passive and vulnerable reclining position would evoke sexual feelings of which they are afraid. Rather than engaging in long discussions about the meaning of their resistances, we let them continue sitting in an upright position and conduct the hypnotic procedures on the chair. Actually this is not much of an impediment, and it is better to respect a person's ego defences at first and let him become aware of them himself rather than confront him with a condition which would constitute a threat to his ego and increase his resistances and his anxieties.

These are exceptions, and I shall here speak of patients with whom analysis is conducted lying on the couch. The patient is asked to make himself comfortable, to relax, and to feel his contact with the couch, to rest his head on the cushion, to feel his back and his buttocks and his legs supported by the couch underneath him. In this way we encourage regression to an infantile sense of being supported and the patient's dependency upon this support, a re-enaction of the primary object relationship, when the infant feels dependent upon his mother and needs her support. We can say that the couch symbolises the mother-infant relationship, and the variety of attitudes which the patient adopts reflects unconscious relationships with his mother. We notice his reactions to the sensation of the couch's support, his acceptance of or resistances against it.

Careful observation of the patient's posture, the way he rests his head upon the pillow, tenses his neck and shoulders, his back and legs, indicates degrees of resistance against dependency and trust. We may, in passing, point out some of his muscular defences, without, however, at this stage attempting any interpretation or entering into discussion about their meaning. We encourage him to feel his whole body, and to speak about his own impressions. After having produced a certain measure of body awareness, we induce hypnosis simply and quickly.

At first the transition from the fairly relaxed state, which I induce before hypnosis, to the hypnotised state is not necessarily very pronounced, and while the patient now has his eyes closed he will sometimes barely notice that he is in a hypnotised state; at other times hypnosis can be quite profound almost immediately. We can observe the transition to the hypnotic state by changes in his breathing rate and tonus.

The first stage of the therapeutic procedure under hypnosis is designed to facilitate hyperawareness of body sensations, enabling the patient to become aware of his neck, shoulders and chest, as well as other areas, such as his arms, legs, feet, hands, his throat, solar plexus, stomach, pelvis and genitals. He may feel tensions or notice that he cannot feel some parts of his body, or that they do not belong to him, or exist outside, independently of him. Indeed, often a wide range of sensations – sometimes quite bizarre – will occur.

He may feel his feet a long way from him, or his arms and hands exceedingly heavy or immobilised, or his head far above his body or floating in the air, either with anxiety or accompanied by sensations of pleasure. All these sensations reported by the patient are of considerable importance for the evaluation of his preconscious state of mind and his body image. As the patient discovers for himself a wide range of unsuspected feelings and sensations, he gradually becomes familiar with unconscious mental and physiological processes. His sense of surprise at his new discoveries will reinforce his interest and lay his ego open, so to speak, to new areas of self awareness.

We move on from the first general and spontaneous observations of his body sensations, and proceed to more specific investigations. I point out to the patient that he can feel any part of his body to which we direct his attention. This too is part of his training in hyperawareness, as well as the beginning of investigations into the roots of his neurotic disturbances.

We once more draw his attention to those areas of his body where he has recognised patterns of unease or pain. I make him, for instance, aware of his hands and stay with them, and examine more fully what they feel and what they are doing. Likewise with other parts of his body.

I then draw his attention to his face, and make him aware of what it feels and what it is doing. If, for instance, he is subject to oral aggressive primacies, as is usually the case with depressive patients, he becomes aware of the tensions in his jaw muscles, and will notice what they are doing. I may draw his attention to his tongue, and notice if it is pressed against the roof of his mouth, as usually happens with people with speech impediments and repressed rage. I also let him feel his teeth and their aggressive impulses. I should mention here that we do not tell patients what they feel, but merely draw attention to certain parts of their body, and let them find out for themselves what goes on there.

Then we move on to the throat, the shoulders, the chest, and observe how they feel and recognise their tensions. I may lay my hand upon his chest and tell him to let it expand and give it more space. Frequently he will recognise that his chest muscles are tight and constricted, that he is shrinking away from the world in order to hide himself in a defensive way.

We then draw his attention to the solar plexus, and make him feel it, notice its tensions and disturbances, and I encourage him to relax and expand it. I often hold his diaphragm, and make him feel a new sense of security, which is frequently accompanied by a kind of gratitude to this new benevolent superego, as presented by the therapist, a sense of relief at being accepted and supported.

We then turn our attention to the stomach, and make him feel what it is doing. In people dominated by anxiety states, the stomach will feel tight and constricted, as if it has no right to receive what it wants. Indeed, the stomach is of particular importance as it contains all the introjections and identifications which we have undergone in our development, or have experienced recently in shocks of rejection or refusals of love; if we are not wanted, we cannot want; if we are not allowed to receive what we want, we cannot expect to be given; we shall feel empty and deprived, and the stomach will act out the sense of emptiness and loneliness by its state of constriction.

We then direct the patient's attention to his legs, to the state of his leg muscles and his feet. If, for instance, in a woman we observe a tightness of the thigh and knee muscles, a posture of holding legs tightly together, we recognise a defence against sexual urges, and we encourage her to feel what her legs are doing. She will frequently recognise them as a kind of barrier against genital feelings, a drawbridge pulled up against them.

I should point out here that the somatic processes which we enable the patient to experience are in fact immensely complex. Tensions and disturbances which we can observe in one part of the body affect other areas. For instance, a tightness of the jaws produces tensions in the neck, the shoulders, the arms; it may spread to the hands, which enact those oral tensions with tensions of the wrist, the knuckles and fingers. The forehead and the eyes may be affected, the stomach drawn upwards, and, in the woman, the vaginal walls may be constricted and the legs tense. While this complicates therapeutic understanding and can be quite confusing, it is fundamentally very simple if we consider that the whole body interacts in a psychobiological unit. The mouth has to grasp, envelop the object of its needs; it has to embrace and suck and chew and bite. The arms and hands replicate the actions of the mouth, and have to grasp and hold and manipulate objects; the throat has to swallow, and the stomach to receive and digest; the legs have to carry the individual towards its desired aim and support the whole organism in its movements.

The way the mouth grasps and envelops and the hands take and manipulate objects is subject to a wide range of variations dependent upon a person's emotional attitudes. He may envelop an object with pleasure, caress it or attack it aggressively; he may be tentative, frightened, insecure or confident. The emotional determinants of these approaches may be chronic or reactive. Fear or aggression, security and confidence may be determined by the actual nature of the object to which he reacts, or by chronic dispositions which reflect a person's character or his neurotic disturbances which are anchored in disturbed object relationships in his childhood. If we notice respiratory impediments – and they are prevalent in neurotics – we teach the patient respiratory relaxation.

A woman, thirty years of age, attractive and intelligent, with the appearance of confident charm, suffered from an acute sense of isolation and inability to establish any satisfactory relationship with men. She was not only shy but anticipated rejection and ridicule to a paranoid degree. Under hypnosis she became aware of painful tensions in her jaws and neck, and when I asked her to relax those tensions by letting herself breathe in and out in a normal and relaxed manner, she had difficulties in letting herself exhale fully. (This is a common phenomenon in neurotic people, for letting oneself breathe out fully, i.e. letting go, produces in them a sense of anxiety which is counteracted by a spasmic block at a particular point of the expiratory process.) When I encouraged her further to let herself exhale and feel her breath coming out, she tightened her shoulders and pulled them up in an almost desperate resistance against letting go. When I asked her what her shoulders were doing, she noticed them tightening up and at the same time holding her breath. She also noticed the tension in her solar plexus 'like a stone upon her stomach which she could not remove'. I also noticed her legs tightening up and her feet being turned inwards. When I asked her to relax her shoulders and solar plexus, she arched her back and recalled that she frequently suffered from backache, which made her feel not only isolated but also that her whole existence was futile and that she was condemned to lead a useless existence leading to frequent desires for suicide. At this stage, I noticed manifestations of sexual anxiety as well as symptoms of retentiveness. I asked her to observe what her anus was doing, and she noticed that it was tight, determined to hold things in. When I asked her to relax her bottom, she became very frightened and at the same time very angry. Her face became red, and her jaws and neck literally swelled up with rage. It was obvious that by asking her to relax herself fully, I threatened her defences: on the one hand she felt threatened by her own libidinous desires which she considered to be bad, and, at the same time, she became overwhelmed by a sense of rage that her desires and her libido were considered to be bad and rejected.

I asked her again to relax, to rest on the couch and tell me why she was afraid. Thereupon her forehead started to twitch, and she became anxious, but eventually relaxed, and I let her fall asleep.

She had previously told me that although she had fallen

in love with a man who wanted to live with her, she could not bring herself to agree, and even though she felt that she desired him, put up all kinds of obstacles to intimacy, indeed, for some apparently unaccountable reason became afraid and completely rejected his advances. While she knew herself to be an attractive woman, she had always spoilt her relationships, causing men to become fed up with her, and she was convinced that the same thing would happen with her present boyfriend. She felt driven by some mysterious force to reject men, and in her current relationship felt guilty about hurting the man, and angry with herself about her utterly ridiculous and self-destructive behaviour. Her relationships with her parents and with her younger brother seemed to be quite conventional and okay, even though she was aware of an absence of warmth and lack of body contact. She could not remember people embracing or cuddling each other, or ever speaking about sex. When she told me about this lack of warmth in her family, I noticed the twitching in her forehead, which had become pronounced under hypnosis. This indicated a conflict between wanting to be loved and accepted, and on the other hand having to hold back her feelings, her conflict of thoughts about right and wrong, and was ultimately an indication of a double bind situation, when parents are represented as kind, loving and considerate and, at the same time, rejective and cold: a split in the superego image. Indeed, she felt the same conflict in her attitude towards men. She knew that she treated them abominably and deserved to be rejected by them but could not help herself, for some uncontrollable power made her behave in this way, even though she was desperate to be loved.

The rejective compulsions, of which the patient was all too painfully conscious, were accompanied by physiological contractions and tensions of which she was not aware. These involuntary processes of the body were the physical expressions of the unconscious, which appeared to be outside the control of the ego but at the same time largely determined its functions.

The next step in the therapy, therefore, was to enable the patient to understand what these involuntary activities meant in psychological terms, and to trace their origins.

3. VISUALISATION: THE UNCONSCIOUS SELF-IMAGE

In order to understand what his bodily sensations and the unconscious activities of his body mean, the patient has to see what his body is doing, and then to discover why. In human beings the visual cortex is the most fully developed, and takes precedence over all other sensory areas. Our perceptual representations are dominated by visual images, and therefore most of our thinking is in pictures; even in conceptual thought processes there is the constant background of visual imagery. All our emotions relate to visual images, and visual images in turn arouse our emotional responses. As Walter Lippman has put it: 'What each does is based not on direct or certain knowledge, but on pictures made by himself or given to him. The way in which the world is imagined determines at any particular moment what men will do.'* Visual images, however, are not merely representations of reality, but frequently give us a distorted picture of reality. We do not respond to reality as such but to our images of reality, and these images are formed by fixations upon fears and desires which dominate our mind, and they have their origins in our past history, often having been formed in childhood and even infancy.

Sometimes a patient, upon becoming aware of certain disturbances of his body functions, will spontaneously recall events which have caused both his psychological as well as somatic conflicts. For instance, a patient suffering from anorexia, who had years of treatment, some of it in hospital,

---

* W Lippmann *Public Opinion* (1922), as quoted by columnist Peter McKay in *The London Evening Standard* of 4. 1. 1993

became aware of a painful tension in her throat, which made it impossible for her to swallow, and a sense of emptiness in her stomach accompanied by a feeling of nausea. She spontaneously recalled a memory of her father looking at her, making her feel a kind of hunger for him as well as rage. She wanted to take him in with her mouth, to suck him and eat him up, so to speak, and at the same time felt rejected and criticised by him. This image made her feel very puzzled as well as evoking a recognition of a familiar feeling of ambivalence towards him. But above all, she recognised feelings of anger, particularly at his frequent criticisms of her. Although this image was very important, it still hid deeper, infantile fantasies. Indeed, she transferred her early oral-sadistic drives, which were originally directed towards her mother, to her father. These things could only be discovered in the course of therapy in depth. I shall return to this patient later.

Another patient, who had suffered from asthma since childhood, recalled memories of panic, of fears that her mother would disappear, accompanied by breathlessness, which she recognised as 'breathless apprehension' of some impending tragedy and loss. She was plagued as a grown-up by a fear that she would never be able to receive what she wanted or accomplish her aims. Although she was an exceptionally intelligent individual, she failed to pass her exams as a medical student. While she was able to connect these memories with her current sense of failure and states of anxiety apprehension, it was left to hypnotic depth therapy to uncover the infantile sources of her current problems, and to cure her of them.

There has been much argument about the sequence in which psychoanalytic therapy should proceed. It is, however, generally accepted now that it is the correct thing to commence with the conflicts which are closest to the surface of the patient's consciousness, and then to proceed gradually to the deeper layers. This has been recognised as in any case the way associations of a patient proceed, and should therefore be encouraged by the analyst. There is, however, another more intense argument, amounting to a clash of opposing schools which frequently adopt dogmatic positions concerning the overriding importance of the ego functions in the development of neurotic symptoms, as opposed to the emphasis upon the unconscious among the more traditional exponents of depth psychology. As I have said, I consider these battles between opposing schools quite unnecessary and even ludicrous, for there is ego psychology as well as the psychology of the deeper levels of the mind, which often operate on the unconscious level.

But there is also a dimension of the ego which is unknown to the patient – the unconscious ego. What the person thinks of himself consciously is not necessarily the same as his unconscious image of himself. These unconscious forms of self-perception are often at sharp variance with the conscious self – they reflect manifestations of the infantile libido, which has become fixated and remained unresolved in the maturation process. They can represent oral-aggressive, anal-retentive, or narcissistic-manic or depressive fixations. The unconscious may be dominated by unresolved rages, tantrums, terrors, devouring-demanding urges and a wide range of libidinous stages. An individual may perceive himself as a tolerant, generous person, while hiding images of himself as a kind of devouring, raging and destructive monster. We can speak, therefore, of a conscious ego image which satisfies the way a person wants to be seen, and an unconscious self-image that is dominated by infantile drives and fantasies.

It is, therefore, his unconscious ego which in the first instance we shall present to the patient. And we do this not by enabling him to think about what this may be, but by enabling him to see it and to feel it, to see his unconscious self-image, and to recognise himself in it. In this way we permit the unconscious self to break through the ego's defences, and find acceptance by it. This, in the first instance, releases considerable amounts of psychic energy which previously were blocked, and in the blocked state acted as a constant threat. But for this act of self-recognition to be possible without intolerable amounts of anxiety, he has to be in a state of security and relaxation, and assured of a positive transference with the hypnotist. It also needs the confidence that one can look at oneself with all one's previously unadmitted characteristics, and, in one's capability of looking at oneself, gain a sense of victory over the enemy within and a release from fear. And this sense of security is provided by the hypnosis.

There are various different techniques we can use for the purpose of providing a visual recognition of the unconscious ego; the one I use most frequently is the 'unconscious-projection mirror'.

In order to deepen the hypnosis, we train the patient's visual sense and intensify pictorial representation. We also utilise all the other senses, hearing, touching, smelling, as well as movement, to induce an increased conviction of the reality of his experiences under hypnosis. We may tell the patient that he is standing on top of a staircase and sees the steps leading down to some (unspecified) place, and there are fifteen steps on the staircase, and then I say, 'Now, you will walk down those steps, as I count to fifteen, and with every count you take a step down, and at the count of fifteen you will come to the bottom of the staircase.' We then say, 'Now!', and begin to count, and when we reach the count of fifteen, we ask him to look around and tell us where he is and what the place looks like. The patient will usually describe an impression of this place, and what he sees there is already of considerable interest, because it represents an environment which symbolises his unconscious state of mind. Often the patient will describe a cellar or a dungeon, where he feels confined and where it is dark and he doesn't know where to go and he feels trapped; or he will see a large hall with people walking around and he doesn't know what to do with himself there; or he feels that he is in a bog, feeling most insecure. The colour tone in which he perceives this place is of importance to the analyst, because he can gauge the state of depression or manic elation, the first being indicated by a sense of darkness, the second by a sense of brightness. We then tell him there is a French window leading out into the garden, and we want him to open this window and walk out into the garden. It is a pleasant, sunny garden, with flowers and bushes and trees, and a lawn, and we want him to walk on the lawn and take his shoes off and feel the grass on the lawn and feel his feet there. And we tell him there is a rose bush and ask him to touch the rose petals with his fingers, and notice the sensations of the rose petals on his fingers. And he will report the sensations of the rose petals. This is meant to induce the sensation of warmth and pleasant, gentle softness, and we ask him to smell the rose and describe its colour. We may also then suggest to him a tree standing at the bottom of the garden, and to go up to it and touch the bark and feel its sensations. Whereas the rose represents the female sensation of gentleness and softness, the tree represents the male strength, the element of roughness, and we shall notice the way he perceives them. Then we ask him to feel at home in this garden and walk around and do whatever he wants to do. We may then want him to lie on the grass, and feel the grass underneath him, and feel his back and his legs and his head resting on the grass, and to relax on it and look at the sky and see the clouds floating by; and he can hear birds and the rustle of the wind, and the grass is freshly mown and he can smell it too. We may ask him to take notice of whatever he is thinking while he is resting there, and speak to us of whatever goes on in his mind. This preliminary exercise is meant to induce a sense of contact with his imaginary surroundings and a sense of security at the same time as his sensorium is activated and he can feel himself. We then ask him to get up again, and to go back to the house into the room behind the French window, and as he looks around to describe the place, we ask him to see a mirror hanging on the wall, and we tell him that it is a very special mirror called 'The unconscious-projection mirror', where he can see his unconscious self as he looks into it. We ask him to describe the mirror at first, and then to step up to it and look into it, and he will see his unconscious self-representation there. At the same time we ask him to remember what he felt earlier in the body analysis, and now to look into the mirror where he can actually see what his unconscious self is doing and what it looks like.

At the end of Chapter 6, I described the patient, Mr G K, whose mother had committed suicide when he was six, and who hated his father, blaming him for his mother's death. During the body analysis, he felt that his periphery was like a tight cage surrounding him and his stomach empty, indeed, that he was hollow inside and it was only the tight frame around him that held him together. When he saw the mirror, he became very anxious, as it was shattered to smithereens. I asked him how the mirror came to be broken, and he said, after some anxious hesitation, that it was he who broke it; he was furious with the mirror, for it would show all the suffering he had experienced since childhood and the futility of his life – nothing but loneliness, grief and rage. I then asked him to repair the mirror and make it whole again and look at himself. He saw himself as a very handsome and charming young man, able to please everybody. When he saw this image, he exclaimed, 'Ah, yes! That's me! Bullshitting everybody and hiding the real me.' The image immediately changed to himself in a state of uncontrolled rage, shouting obscenities, waving his arms in an extremely aggressive manner, being literally 'hopping mad', hitting and biting people, clearly wanting to kill them. He laughed when he saw this image, but then it became rigid. It became totally immobilised, with his arms held close to his body, and his legs standing to attention. He then moved his arm to perform a military salute – 'Ah! That's again another version of my defensive bullshitting. I don't believe it, and if they don't believe it, I kill them.' And then he saw himself crying and collapsing in an agony of defeat and self-pity. I then said, 'Come on! Cut out the posturing and let's look at him how he really is.' He then saw himself walking about in a dark street, looking for something, with an expression of hunger and yearning and clutching a bottle. He saw himself as an empty person, always wanting something but never getting any satisfaction. He ran up to an apple tree, and tore some apples off, and greedily put them into his mouth, but even as he put them into his mouth, the apples disappeared, and he was left desperately hungry and empty again. The scene then changed spontaneously, and he was six years old, in a fairground. He looked at all the booths, and heard the fairground organs playing, and was excited by all the noise and colour around him; but he was looking for his mother, and he knew he could not find her. Then the scene changed again, and he was his grown-up self, not trusting anybody, as everybody was in a conspiracy to deny his real self, in effect, denying his mother. He was drinking heavily then, as indeed he had become an alcoholic, and he described that as he was drinking bottle after bottle, he felt, on the one hand, absolutely full, till his body could not take any more, and, at the same time, still desperately thirsty and empty, and there was no solution. He was then lying on his bed in a kind of hopeless stupor, and then saw himself on a bed as a child of six years old again, shortly after his mother died, being desperately ill. I then asked him to look at this sick child, and to understand what was really the matter with him. He saw that the child was immobilised, his whole body rigid, his eyes motionless, as if he wanted the world to stand still. Indeed, he wanted to be dead, like his mother.

In actual fact, he became very ill after his mother died, would hardly eat anything, repeatedly suffering from stomach colics, apparently unable to speak or to move, and his metabolic rate reduced to dangerously low levels. After about six months he recovered physically, and he decided to adopt the role of a good boy, coping with his destructive and self-destructive rage, by developing a split, schizoid personality. His rage had to be hidden behind his charming and pleasing exterior, and was prevented from finding expression in public. It therefore became projected upon the world, and produced paranoid fantasies, with the conviction that fate and everybody, whom he had any dealings with, were persecuting him. His own repressed hatreds were represented by the world around him, and he saw himself as its victim. This in turn, however, produced fits of rage which could only be stilled by compulsive drinking later in life.

Although he had been told of his severe illness after his mother died, an illness which set the pattern of his psychic structure, he never actually remembered it. He recognised the scene at the fairground as a real experience, even though he had completely forgotten it. Indeed, he used to complain that he could not remember anything of his childhood, and that he had no memory at all of his mother. It was, therefore, the next step in the therapy to make him remember his mother and, so to speak, reunite him with her, and make him feel that he belonged, that he had a real identity and was not an alien, a non-person in a world which had rejected him, as he then rejected it.

4. AGE REGRESSION: RE-EXPERIENCING THE PAST

It is one of the corner-stones of psychoanalytic therapy that a patient cannot be freed from his neurotic disturbances unless he is able to remember and above all to re-experience the emotional trauma which has led to the formation of his symptoms. As Winnicott has remarked: 'There can be no successful end to the treatment unless the depth of the patient's emotional disturbance has been reached, and unless he has really experienced what he is frightened of. What then is the nature of real experience? What is the nature of the understanding and insight which leads to the transformation of that which was unconscious into consciousness?'*

---

* D W Winnicott 'Fear of Breakdown' (*International Review of Psychoanalysis Vol 1 1974 pp103-107*

It is obviously not enough to be informed of those long-forgotten traumatic events unless one can re-live and emotionally re-experience them. To quote Erich Fromm: 'There is no doubt that in the early years of his psycho-analytic investigations Freud shared the conventional, rational belief that knowledge is a matter of intellect and rational theory. He thought that it would be enough to explain to the patient why certain developments have taken place in his psyche, and to let him know what the analyst has found in his unconscious. This kind of knowledge, which usually goes by the name of interpretation, was expected to bring about the desired transformation in the patient. But soon Freud and other analysts had to discover the truth of Spinoza's statement that intellectual knowledge can only promote a spiritual transformation insofar as it is at the same time an emotional experience. It became obvious that intellectual knowledge by itself cannot effect such a change. To discover the unconscious, it is not enough to engage in intellectual activity, but it necessitates an emotional reliving of previously repressed experiences and traumas, and this can rarely find expression in words.'*

While the Neo-Freudians and, in particular, the object-relation therapists attempt to bring those repressed emotional experiences to the surface through the patient's relationship to the therapist and analysis of the transference, we attempt to go direct to the actual object of the patient's disturbed relationships. The patient is led back to the situations in his past life which have turned out to be traumatic and responsible for the development of his neurotic disturbances, to see himself in those situations and to actually experience the intense emotions aroused by them. We are not merely speaking of recall of forgotten memories but of reliving the reality of his traumatic disturbances.

Mr G K again looked into the mirror at his next session, and saw himself standing there quite rigid, downcast and

---

* Erich Fromm *Zen Buddhism and Psychoanalysis* (NY, 1960)

altogether miserable. I asked him to feel what this fellow in the mirror feels. He immediately felt his body very tight all over, 'front and back touching each other, and there is nothing in between, as if there is no inside; panic, everything is panicking, everything is tense and pulling inwards, all contraction and no release.'

I then initiated age regression by asking him to step into the mirror, get hold of the fellow's hand and ask him to take him back in time to when he was a child, and to meet his mother. After a few seconds he saw himself in the house where he lived as a child:

'I am crying. I am not allowed to look for mummy. I am very frightened. I can't find her.'

'How old are you?'

'I think I am six, and I am alone in the house. Mother is not there.'

I get him to describe what the house looks like, and then I tell him to go back in time to two weeks earlier.

'I am with my mother. She looks very frightened, and I am very frightened. I know there is something wrong, there is a despair. She says we (my sister and I) are going to leave home to stay with daddy. I do not want to know, I don't want to leave her. We are on the Isle of Wight. I can see the house and I can see mummy. She wants me to go with my father and stepmother. I won't go. I just switched off. I tell her: "If you don't want me, I don't want to be with anybody." But we were taken away, and I never saw mummy again. She died, and I refused to live.'

His mother committed suicide a few days after this episode. She was taken to be buried, while the children were left in the house with a neighbour and then taken to their father and his lady friend, with whom he lived at the time and married shortly afterwards. As soon as he came to his father's house he fell ill. He refused to be there, to live there.

In our explorations into the unconscious we soon become aware that the traditional classifications, such as depressive, manic or manic-depressive, paranoid, hysteric, compulsive or schizoid, tend to be over-simplifications, which suit the therapist's need to bring some order into the often chaotic and apparently contradictory mental processes experienced and reported by the patient. As a matter of fact, the data produced tend to cut across the diagnostic categories, and while it is true that certain symptom systems predominate, they are merely the end result of a complex chain of mental processes. Thus, psychic processes which at first appear non-reconcilable interact in one psychic disorder. Indeed, contradictory drives can be observed in practically all patients, for, after all, irresolvable conflict is the chief characteristic of neurosis. In our depth analytic procedure we constantly encounter such contradictions and paradoxes, and we refrain from imposing upon patients interpretations dominated by our diagnostic categories. One has to dispense as far as possible with diagnostic preconceptions; not only should we guard against giving interpretations before the patient practically arrives at them himself, but also against premature interpretations in our own mind. I almost never give interpretations, but allow the patient to come to them himself and present them to me as his token of discovery, as his communication of surprise and his feeling of release from his emotional burden.

After the session in which Mr G K remembered his mother and experienced her sorrow and his own despair, he arrived much more confident and at ease. He had felt shaken for a few days and cried a lot. But then a transformation took place in his mind. The anxiety and the rage which had dominated him all those years lifted, and he was amazed that he had nothing really to worry about. When he woke up in the mornings, he expected as usual that some heavy worry and depression would descend upon him, a sense of doom and outrage, but it was not there, and he felt free of a burden that had weighed upon him practically all his life. This, he said, was an overwhelming new experience, and he was very pleased with himself. I let him talk about his new self and the pleasure he felt about this transformation.

In the following session he told me that he had made the acquaintance of a young lady and become very attracted to her. He tried to tell her what he felt but realised that, despite his strong feelings, he could not find words for them; they belonged to a world he had not experienced ever since he could remember and to his astonishment did not find the proper language for them. I then hypnotised him and asked him to observe what his body felt. He immediately reported that there was now room in his body between his back and his front, that his chest felt much more free and he could feel a pleasant sense of excitement in his stomach. His lips felt sensitive, very wanting; they wanted to reach out for something pleasant with a loving feeling and that made him feel good and happy. He realised that previously his face felt like a mask, his lips under-nourished, mistrustful and hard, and his solar plexus used to tighten up like a knot.

He then spoke about his previous attitudes to women and sex: 'I considered everything to do with sex as false, as a lie. I did not trust it. I did not feel my penis real; it was there to prove my power, to assert myself over women or to please them and make a great impression upon them, but I could not relate to it. Sex was like some kind of duty.' Since his teens he had many sexual encounters, in fact, he was obsessed by sex without being emotionally involved. It was a way of conquering women, but he hated them because they could not give him what he really wanted, and in the end they would let him down. He was dominated by a phallic-aggressive libido, 'cold sex', as he put it, and felt that he attacked women aggressively but always felt dissatisfied and empty afterwards: 'Now everything is opening up in me, and I can feel deep feelings, and my penis feels part of me. When it's excited I am not separate from it but it is me who is excited. And I want women to have powerful feelings for me, to feel what I feel, and that makes me feel good, that makes me happy.'

I then instructed him to go back in time to his early childhood. His face became animated and slightly flushed with an expression of pleasure, and he reached out with his arms as if to embrace someone. He then saw his mother as a young woman looking at him happily, and he felt her warmth and her love. She held him to her body and embraced him, and he enacted his happiness like a small child. He then cried a little, but it was a crying of a newly discovered happiness. I let him experience his feelings and describe what he saw. He recognised and described the room where he lived as an infant and as a child, but his emotions were so powerful that he largely communicated to me what he felt with his body gestures, in fact behaving like a happy little child. In following sessions he spoke of many situations during his early childhood which were dominated by a good relationship with his mother and his sister. At first his father barely figured. He hardly knew him and did not seem to react to his occasional appearances. However, he began to notice that whenever father appeared, the atmosphere changed. Mother became distant, cold, held back, and the warmth went out of her. He realised that she was frightened of father, and there was panic in her face. The scene changed from happiness to being completely distraught: 'When she is with me she is happy, but it is as if she is doing it behind father's back.'

This conflict which mother experienced and which he was aware of even as a baby, produced a profound split in his personality. On the one hand he received the most exquisite sense of pleasure, and on the other he was apprehensive, mistrustful and prone to panic attacks. He felt his mother's fear of his father, which often showed by the panic in her face. On one occasion when he recalled these conflicts, I observed half-jokingly that he had not changed much since then, and he nodded gravely, with a sense of recognition, and laughed. (I should mention here that important moments of recognition are accompanied by relief and laughter.)

He then saw himself as a two-year old running around the place. 'Mother looks at me with love. She loves me, but she is crying. I am too much for her. I am overcompensating, I want to make her happy. I want to show that I love her, so that she should not be miserable and frightened of Daddy.'

His relationship to his father and other men in position of some authority then became the major topic of interest. When he looked at himself in the mirror he saw that he was not holding himself in, his eyes are clear and they look at people directly, whereas previously they were somewhat veiled and shifty. He is rather cocky and self-assertive without trying too hard, his movements are fluid and he approves of himself. In discussion with his employers he is now straightforward, without anxiety or hidden anger, and he uses his brain effectively. He is relaxed and does not feel the pressure of outrage, nor does he have to defeat other men at all costs. In other words, his paranoid obsessions have lifted. And then he remembers that he was frightened, absolutely terrified of his father, but did not understand why. He also noticed that father felt unsure and frightened. 'He is completely frightened of me, I always felt he did not want to know me. When I showed off and talked about myself he used to get deeply embarrassed, and that made me embarrassed and angry. But now I want to relate to him as two mature men. I can now understand his predicament, namely his guilt feelings towards me and my sister, which made him embarrassed and withdrawn. In fact, our very existence was a constant accusation about what he did to my mother, and it made him defensive and sarcastic and intolerant. I can see him now as a fellow with all kinds of faults and many difficulties and no longer as an implacable, larger than life authority. I no longer depend on him and I can be myself.'

The task of weaning themselves from a negative super-ego is a problem for all patients. But as they regain a measure of self-acceptance, they are able to judge their parents and other authority figures for their merits and their faults. One can say that they are released from the grip of the introjected primary objects, and their libido, which was largely directed by the internal authority can be channelled into an ego ideal which they learn to develop with some occasional tribulations and anxieties: they can freely ask themselves what they want to be and how they want to see themselves. Indeed, a successful analysis produces the challenge and the opportunity of freedom and enables a person to exercise it. Patients thus emerge from a prison from which they have tried to escape through a whole host of secondary or substitute drives, such as aggression, defiance, guilt, self-punishment, paranoid mistrust as well as destructive and self-destructive urges. I have described this process in some detail in my book *The Unknown Self*, and here I want to provide some further examples of the nature of libidinous primacies, how individuals react to them and how they become fixated upon these reaction formations. These processes of fixation usually take place at a very early age, belonging to that 'other country, that dark continent' to which our conscious mind has no access. Freud has provided a somewhat sketchy map of that continent of the mind, from the outside, as it were, and we want to enter it, see it from the inside, and participate in its life; but this will entail entering into the infant's earliest experiences practically from birth.

8 Going to the Roots

1. EMPATHY AND UNDERSTANDING

In the therapeutic method we employ, we enable the patient to recall and re-experience the decisive situations which are responsible for his psychic disturbance, and by his understanding of the chief factors of his neurosis he enables us to understand them also. In other words, we do not need to impose constructions and explanations upon the patient, nor do we challenge him with our interpretations, but we are guided by his insights and accompany him in the process of understanding. Indeed, it is the interaction between the patient's and the therapist's understanding of his neurosis, the therapist's acknowledgement of the traumatic experiences, which helps to release the patient from his repressions and lays the foundations for his cure. But it is not only the cognitive co-operation between therapist and patient, but above all the therapist's emotional empathy, his participation in the patient's fear and conflict which plays an important part in the curative process; as the patient feels that the analyst can accept the conflicts and fears which he had to hide from the world and from himself, he begins to feel that he can accept them also. It is not merely what the analyst says, and his show of superior knowledge and interpretative ability, but his emotional participation which transforms the patient's sense of isolation into a sense of being accepted and acknowledged as a person.

The depth analytic therapist, therefore, has to be able to show his humanity and his emotional responses and to share them with his patient in the same way as the infant can feel the mother's feelings and her emotional attitude long before words are available. However, a mother's words of love and understanding are often contradicted by her real emotions and thoughts, of which a child is all too aware, and produce what R D Laing has called the double-bind, with devastating effects upon the child's ego formation, tending to produce a split in its own psyche, as it has experienced a split, a contradiction in its mother's psyche. This effect of double-bind is often produced in therapy, when the therapist makes statements and interpretations without emotional participation, without emotional understanding. In other words, the communication of empathy between patient and therapist is of crucial importance, as it is important in the relationship of the infant with his mother. And do we not all, even as grown-ups, wonder, often with some anxiety, what people really mean behind what they are saying? And how often do we hear patients complain that their parents do not really understand them, however much they say the correct things or what they imagine are the correct things to say, and how often does one hear patients declare that, despite all his interesting interpretations and reconstructions, the therapist has not really understood them? For after all, 'understanding' does not merely mean the correct intellectual recognition of another person's thoughts and feelings, but also emotional empathy. This also enables us to understand the patient's emotional expression in his 'body language'. If, therefore, the therapist can 'understand' a patient's emotional experiences, he will be able at least to some extent to gauge the meaning of his bodily expression and his neurotic symptoms. Empathy means 'feeling with another person', and in our emotional participation with the emotions of the patient we not only understand him as a grown-up but also the child in him, its desires, its fears and rages. But of course it is not enough for the therapist to understand the patient, the patient also has to understand himself.

It is, as I have pointed out, the task of depth analytic therapy to enable the patient to rediscover those areas of his psyche which can be considered the domain of the unconscious proper; it is the long-forgotten past which appears to belong to another country and which, if he were told about it, he would not recognise as his own, not part of himself. If we intend to uncover the roots of his pathology, we have to make it possible for the patient to recognise himself in the strange world of his unconscious.

2. A CASE OF ANOREXIA NERVOSA.

I referred earlier to the patient who suffered from anorexia and had about three years of intermittent hospital treatment before she came to see me. Despite all her efforts, she could not get food down her throat, and if she tried really hard she would vomit almost straightway. She could nibble little bits of bread or drink liquid, such as milk or orange-ades, as long as there were no traces of food substance in it, such as found in soups, for instance. The only soup she could drink had to be thin or clear soup. We found that she was above all frightened of biting things; she could swallow as long as she did not have to bite.

In the body analysis she felt a 'queer sensation' in her teeth which frightened her, and she realised that they were generally in a clenched position and her jaw muscles very rigid. Her nose was tight and her forehead frowning. When she directed her attention to her throat, she noticed that it was contracted and tense, and for what appeared to be the first time she realised that it was constantly painful in its rigidity. Her chest was contracted, drawn in, as she put it, and above all her solar plexus clenched and drawn upwards. I have mentioned earlier the importance of the solar plexus as the controller of the intake process, but unlike many other patients, who eat a lot, stuff themselves in order to fill up the stomach which is desensitised and feels constantly empty and then have to reject the food which the solar plexus refuses to accept, this patient's tensions in her throat and solar plexus made it impossible to accept food altogether. Her legs were fairly rigid but tended to want to kick, which she inhibited for it caused her anxieties, with the result that they were at the same time restless and nervous, unfeeling and lifeless. She had fairly large lips which, however, felt hard, a wide mouth that appeared to want to attack and devour, accompanied by a constant frown which indicated guilt feelings and expectation of punishment. When I introduced her to the unconscious projection mirror, she at first did not want to look into it, but after I used various stratagems, such as making her walk past the mirror and just glance into it, stratagems designed to confuse the defence mechanism and to catch her by surprise, she saw herself as a witch, emaciated, bony, long claws, and with large teeth about to attack. She felt frightened by this image, and it remained static and frozen. This frightening image had to be delibidinised and denied any movement, for she could not accept the libidinous drives behind it. I then made her touch this immobilised spectre, made her feel it and talk to it, and, to make it come alive, humanise it, so to speak, and allow the patient to feel that her ego has some dominance over this image, and to encourage some understanding, even a sense of empathy with it. This enabled her to recognise something of herself in this figure. When the patient started to touch this monster, which at first appeared black or grey against a dark background, it acquired some colour and became more lifelike. But then it started to snap and grip in a most frightening manner, but I encouraged the patient to stay with it, not to be afraid, and to tell the monster to look around and to watch what it is looking at. This witch-like female image then looked at her parents' bedroom and saw her father walking about in his pyjamas. The patient then saw herself as a little girl of about two and a half, looking fixedly at the fly-opening in father's pyjamas in order to see his penis:

'I can now see his penis through the slit in his pyjamas, but it is red and there is blood on it.' This was obviously a screen memory where an unconscious fantasy is superimposed upon the visual perception. It indicates an oral-aggressive urge to attack the object of her libidinous interest. But I said nothing of this to the patient.

'I am very disturbed and frightened and astonished, but also very excited.' She then saw a large shadow image of her father, with herself looking at his penis.

'I want to take it in my mouth, and I am biting it. I want to take it into myself, and I can feel its flesh and I am chewing at it, and I can feel the blood.' She then spontaneously returned to her present age, and reflected that she had these fantasies not merely as a child but ever since she could remember. Her sexual drive was dominated by the sensation of chewing the man's flesh and feeling the flesh in her teeth. When she spoke about this, I could see her mouth masticating and salivating and eyes expanding with excitement and horror at the same time.

I then woke her up, and she quite easily remembered the scenes and thoughts under hypnosis, and acknowledged her cannibalistic urges. She spoke about these things in a matter of fact way, as if she had known about them all along. However, at one point she shuddered, and experienced spasms in her throat and her stomach, and her legs started kicking slightly, but she seemed to be undisturbed and wanted to tell me her thoughts.

In subsequent sessions she was preoccupied with her relationship with her father in childhood and early adolescence, and described many scenes of ambivalence towards him. He used to be very critical of her, often attacked her verbally, but behind his critical attitudes she felt a kindness and even love, which he had to hide, and he became aggressive towards her, as if he regretted having to deny his feelings. She was very disappointed with his attitudes and very angry with him. Indeed her first signs of anorexia happened after she had a row with him on coming home late. She recalled a scene when he bent over her snarling and furious and she shuddered at seeing his angry face.

After these recollections which were to a large extent situations overshadowed by her own fantasies, she began to eat and even – with some apprehension at first –

developed a taste for meat and put on weight. But these improvements would have been unreliable and probably transitory because we still did not understand how her sadistic urges towards her father originated. In order to consolidate her improvement, it was clear to me that we had to go back to the origins of her oral-sadistic libido, to the experiences and sensations at her mother's breast.

The observations of Karl Abraham, Melanie Klein and Helene Deutsch have shown that little girls transfer their oral libido to their father at a very early age. Following the lead of Karl Abraham, Melanie Klein has drawn our attention to the fact that soon after girls are weaned from the breast they turn towards their father, replacing the breast with the penis as an object of oral desire. Melanie Klein and many other child analysts since then have also observed that these oral desires are accompanied by genital impulses. Under the dominance of oral primacy the father's penis is an object which the girl wants to suck and incorporate via the mouth, and these urges and fantasies are accompanied by vaginal sensations and spasms. Helene Deutsch has pointed out that already very early on in life the small girl, in taking her father as the object of her affection next in order to her mother, directs towards him a great part of that true sexual libido attached to the oral zone with which she has cathexed her mother's breast, since in that phase of her development her unconscious equates her father's penis with her mother's breast for giving suck.

The stimulations of the oral sphere in the act of sucking arouse vaginal sensations, and there is no doubt about the similarity of the oral and vaginal activities and the inter-acting stimulation which occurs between the two. The lips which reach forward when they become aware of the breast, the desire to open the mouth to receive the nipple in response to the libidinous sensations emitted from it, exercise a stimulus on the vagina, and it will make equivalent involuntary movements. If we bear this fundamental correlation between the two organs in mind, it will explain many problems in the psychology of women which have previously remained shrouded in obscurity. If what I have called the embracing and sucking aspect of the oral libido finds responses and satisfactions at the breast, the latter will appear as a loving and responsive object. The memories of the good sensations and good image of it will produce the image of the good penis and good father, and the girl will turn to him with trust as a new object of her oral needs, which have been disrupted by the shock of weaning.

'If a large part of her oral libido has been transformed into aggressive-cannibalistic drives, these will most likely be directed towards the penis. In the same manner as the infant projects its own aggressive instincts on to the breast, and sees it as bad and dangerous, the girl will think of the penis as having extremely dangerous attributes. She will be tied to this dangerous object by the bonds of a sado-masochistic cathexis which arouses both her excitement as well as her fears.'* It is, therefore, our task to enable the patient to re-experience the sensations and emotions at the mother's breast. For it is not enough to know that an infant's relationship to its mother was dominated by aggressive-cannibalistic urges; we want to understand how they originated, why the yearning for love and security was transformed into aggression and anger.

3. A PERSON'S EARLIEST EXPERIENCE OF LIFE

If we intend to explore the period of early infancy, and by that I mean the infant's sensations of the mother's breast, we once more have to rely on the somatic processes, the sensations and reflexes of the body. It is of this period of infancy that we can truly say that the psyche is in the body, or to put it the other way round, the sensations of the body are psychological experiences. And it is particularly the lips and the solar plexus which are the first information systems available to the new-born.

---

* G Frankl *The Unknown Self* (Open Gate Press, 1990) pp102-103

I want here to say a few words about the theoretical concepts which have directed my attention to the post-natal experiences of the infant and encouraged me to search for a way to enable a patient to re-experience the sensations, the dramas, pleasures and tragedies of the first few days and weeks of its existence, and to observe their influence upon its later development. Indeed, I have again and again found, not without some astonishment, that the roots of neurotic or even psychotic disturbances can to a great extent be found in those early encounters with the mother's breast.

When the child is expelled from its accustomed universe of the womb, large amounts of libido flow into the lips, and they become highly sensitised. It is important to realise that the infant is not merely a passive recipient of the mother's milk when the nipple is put into its mouth, but that it is imbued with an instinct to reach out towards the nipple as soon as it feels its contact. Its lips are an orientation and explorative organ, similar to that of a monkey or ape. As soon as it feels the sensations of the mother's body and, in particular, as it receives the libidinous sensations of the breast, its lips reach out towards the nipples and the sucking reflex emerges. It is no exaggeration to say that the new-born infant sees and knows with its lips, that they are the centre of all attention, judgement and gratification, and very quickly it becomes aware of the mother's feel and of her libidinous responses through the nipple. Just as much as the infant's centre of attention and orientation lie in its lips – the most highly libidinous part of its body – so the mother's nipples become the centre of its world, the focus of its needs. And furthermore, the mother's nipples are not only the main object for the child, but the mother's central area of communication with the child. The mother's breast becomes indeed the baby's whole universe.

It seems that nature has provided us with a signalling system for the communication of libido in the form of pleasure sensations. We reach out for warmth and libidinous gratification, and we are made aware of it by a feeling of pleasure. But we also want to give out libido to another person whom we love, and one of the most important of these giving urges is that of the mother to the child. In the interaction between mother and child, it feels pleasure upon receiving the mother's libido, but it also perceives the mother's pleasure. If we notice that the object responds with pleasure to our desire, and feel that we give pleasure to the object upon whom we depend, then we are important and wanted, and our desire is good. Then we incorporate the other person's pleasure into ourselves and are pleased with ourselves. The object then is a good object and we are good subjects, and we have a good feeling of ourselves. There is also no doubt that the sensations of pleasure we feel also have an erotic or sexual component. The pleasure sensations aroused by the baby as it stimulates the mother's nipple also stimulates a wider range of erotic sensations in her, often accompanied by vaginal sensations, and conversely, one can frequently observe genital sensations with erections in male infants, and this also occurs in the form of vaginal sensations in baby girls.

However, these fundamental processes can be easily disturbed, particularly by mothers who suffer from erotic inhibitions, pleasure anxiety and various forms of dissatisfaction and resentment. The basic and apparently simple act of mothering can undergo an enormously wide range of disturbances and complications among human beings, with important repercussions in the psychological development of the child.

Melanie Klein has repeatedly stressed the overriding importance of the infant's relationship to its mother's breast as the foundation for a person's character development. In her pioneering work on child analysis she has shed much new light on the remote and forgotten periods of our life: 'Throughout my work I have attributed fundamental importance to the infant's first object relation – the relation to the mother's breast and to the mother – and have drawn the conclusion that if this primal object, which is introjected, takes root in the ego with relative security, the basis for a satisfactory development is laid. Innate factors contribute to this bond. Under the dominance of oral impulses the breast is instinctively felt to be the source of nourishment and therefore, in a deeper sense, of life itself. The mental and physical closeness to the gratifying breast in some measure restores, if things go well, the lost pre-natal unity with the mother, and the feelings of security that go with it. This largely depends on the infant's capacity to cathect sufficiently the breast or its symbolic repre-sentative, the bottle. In this way the mother is turned into a loved object. It may well be that having been part of the mother in the pre-natal stage contributes to the infant's innate feeling that there exists something outside him, something that will give him all he needs and desires. The good breast is taken in and becomes part of the ego, and the infant who was first inside the mother now has the mother inside himself. I would not assume that the breast is to the child merely a physical object. The whole of his instinctual desires and his unconscious fantasies imbue the breast with qualities going far beyond the actual nourish-ment it affords. We find in analysis of our patients that the breast, as the good object, is the prototype of eternal goodness, inexhaustible patience and generosity as well as of creativeness. It is these fantasies and instinctual needs that so enrich the primal object that remain the foundation for hope, trust and belief in goodness.'*

We notice that Melanie Klein draws attention to the fact that it is not only the nourishment, the milk, which is all important; it is the sensation of the libido, the mother's pleasure sensations, which the infant needs to feel in order to experience a secure and joyful relationship to the mother and with it, later, to the outside world. However, the infant experiences a wide variety of sensations, and the inborn urges for libidinous gratification and pleasure can turn to anxiety, inhibition and aggressiveness. The good object, invested with a potential for pleasurable satisfaction, can

---

* Melanie Klein *The Psychoanalysis of Children* (Hogarth, 1932)

turn into a bad object and make it impossible for the child to relax with a sense of pleasurable gratitude, leaving it in a state of anxiety, anger and restlessness.

To return to the methods we employ in order to reach those early stages. During his body analysis, we shall already have taught the patient to be aware of any part of his body to which we direct his attention, and observed the sensations and attitudes of his lips. We now tell the patient that we want to go back to his infancy and find out what happened in his encounter with the mother's breast. Having hypnotised him, we again draw his attention to his face, let him feel it, and ask him to feel his lips as a baby, when they are enormously sensitive and he perceives everything with his lips and they are the centre of all his experience. We then ask him how he feels his lips, and he will tell us that they are in fact much bigger and very sensitive indeed. We then tell him that he now feels his mother's nipple coming to his lips, that he can feel it now, and to tell us what it feels like. We may mention that of course the baby can't talk, but that it has a wide range of very powerful experiences and we want these experiences to be put into words. With intellectual patients we may explain that while the baby's speech cortex is not yet developed, we can use his grown-up cortical system in order to translate the infant's sensations into words. We may even give a short description of the neuro-physiological processes involved, but this is often not necessary because the sensations will in most cases be spontaneous. If the patient hesitates and does not know how to express his sensations, we may prompt him by asking whether the nipple feels warm or cold, rough or smooth, hard or soft, large or small, and so on. We observe his facial reactions and the responses of his mouth and his lips.

Our anorexic patient at first looked somewhat puzzled and unsure, almost indifferent, and then her face flushed, she became somewhat anxious and reported that the nipple is smooth but there is no feel in it, that it seems indifferent and cold, like it does not really belong there: 'I don't know what I am supposed to do with it, and it does not seem to care. It feels indifferent towards me, and there is no pleasure, no good feeling there. I am getting frightened. Although it is fairly hard, it also feels limp, as if mother is pulling back. Perhaps she does not want me there.' There was by now considerable anxiety in the patient, she tensed up her whole body and she appeared to become immobilised, not knowing what to do. After a while, I tell her that the sucking reflex will now take over, and to tell me what is happening. Almost with reluctance she started to suck, her forehead frowning and her neck tight: 'I can now feel the milk coming out. It tastes sour and I don't like it, I don't want it. What is mother doing to me? She does not like me. My lips are tense and my throat is painful, and I feel revolted by this thing that is coming into me. In fact, my whole body is revolted, and I'm struggling against it.' (I should mention here that taste is the most basic and earliest of all sensations and can be considered the primary information system, certainly in apes and humans, concerning the suitability of an object for its introjection, whether it can be taken in or has to be rejected. However, things become complicated as the animal, and particularly the human infant, is entirely dependent upon the object, i.e. the breast and the milk, for its survival, and a battle between hunger and rejection, desire and disgust may ensue. Then the nourishment which tastes bad, i.e. is bad if taken in and swallowed, continues to be bad inside and the infant feels bad.)

I then asked her to feel the milk going down her throat and into the stomach: 'It is not going down, it is all over my face, but I'm hungry, so I push it down my throat.' I ask her to feel her stomach: 'My stomach is tense, pushed upwards, tight and empty. My legs are squeezing up against it.' In fact I could see her feet turning inwards and the toes curling up. Her face was flushed with a tight mask of resentment. There is no doubt she must have been a very difficult baby to feed and a source of despair to her mother.

I asked the patient to move forward in time, about two

months: 'I feel the nipple, it is withdrawn. It tries to get away, but I now put my lips firmly around it: Yes! I have got the measure of it, perhaps. I am squeezing the nipple with my lips and my tongue, and if she withdraws I squeeze it harder. I press and squeeze to make myself feel it. Milk comes out and goes into my stomach, but it all feels angry – not good – but at least I get something!' In a subsequent session she suddenly feels that something is exploding in her head, and she is very frightened. I asked her to tell me slowly what is going on: 'I am very frightened. I am shaking all over, I am in a terrible rage. Mother has pushed me away. She is angry, and I feel my teeth under my gums and I attack the nipple, I bite it. I want to bite right through it so that she cannot disappear. Only when I bite it can I feel it.' Indeed, I notice that a tension has spread from her lips to the jaws, and a kind of snarling movement appears revealing her teeth. It seems that the explosion in her head was an outburst of rage and sadism, previously controlled by a tense musculature. At the same time this breakthrough of the sadistic libido produced great fear, a sensation of a frightening explosion. We can say that she was breaking through her own armour in a fit of rage, which would have been seen as a tantrum or convulsion in the baby. I should mention that a number of grown-up patients have reported this sensation of an explosion in their heads, which we could trace to a fit of rage which burst through their ego defences or, in Reichian terms, exploded their armour. This patient seems to have hurt her mother's breast, and she was transferred to the bottle: 'I now feel the nipple is different, it's rubbery, but the milk comes out now more easily. But it feels lifeless, indifferent. I am now indifferent, and the only pleasure I get is from biting at it; it does not seem to mind, it does not get upset, but at least I can do what I like with it. I play with it and chew it and bite it; it is not very good but it does not mind.' I then ask her to grasp it with her hands and hold it. 'Oh! It's a bottle, it's smooth and lifeless. It feels cold but it isn't really cold. What is the matter with mother? What has happened to her? I reach out to her. I can feel her now, she does not seem to care, she is there but she does not feel me. She is indifferent. She is talking to people, and her mind is not with me. I can hear her talking and she is not looking at me. I am trying to feel indifferent but I don't like it.'

It is interesting to note that when she was speaking earlier of her feelings and fantasies about her father, the mother hardly figured. When I asked about the mother, she appeared as a shadowy, distant figure. The patient's libido seems to have withdrawn from her mother.

This may account for the indifferent, almost impersonal way in which she spoke about her cannibalistic fantasies towards her father as if she had known about them all along and was quite content to talk to me about them without any feeling. There is no doubt that she had adopted a stubborn character trait, a kind of fatalism which made her neurotic syndrome seem inevitable and which she, or anybody else, could do nothing about. This may also account for the lack of success of her hospital treatment. When I asked her at a subsequent session whether she told her doctors about her fantasies, she reacted by saying that she certainly did not, and in any case they never asked.

This patient introjected her mother's indifference which prevented her from showing her libidinous desires and seeking gratification for them. To find an outlet, the libido had to break through the armour of indifference by outbursts of rage, which in turn had to be repressed. Thus a self-perpetuating circle of indifference, secrecy and sadism imprisoned this patient with a sense of inevitability. By the time she was fourteen she had developed a withdrawn and mistrustful personality. Although she was interested in the arts and could draw well, she never, or with the greatest reluctance, showed her drawings to others and when she occasionally went to the theatre she did so on her own. She hardly ever showed any interest in boys, being isolated within her own preconscious sadistic fantasies. On the conscious level she asked for nothing and gave nothing. Her whole personality was dark and stubborn.

At one of her hypnotic sessions dealing with the infant's relationship with her mother I asked her to look at her mother. She seemed reluctant to do so, but with some prompting she saw her. Upon looking at her face she saw that it was tight, her lips unyielding, like a trap, the eyes withdrawn and not looking at the patient, they looked hard and hostile. I could see the patient visibly shrinking away and getting quite rigid as she struggled against being sick. She cried a little but again held herself together trying not to give in to her emotions. I then said to her: 'You quite obviously and naturally don't want your mother to be like that. I shall now count to five and you will see your mother as you really, deep down want her to be, as a good mother in order to feel good.' She looked intensely and after a while a smile appeared on her face. 'She is looking at me and pleasure shows in her face. She is pleased with me and she likes me. I make her feel good and she is happy to have me. Her face is now open and at ease, her eyes smiling and this good feeling comes over to me. I make a giggling noise and she laughs. Now she picks me up and holds me and it feels really good. I can now feel secure and at ease. Everything is much brighter and she looks young and happy.' I let her talk about her new feelings and obviously there was an expansive sensation both in her mind and in her body. I asked her to feel the breast and the milk. 'Ooh, ooh, it feels lovely and I suck and the milk is sweet and it goes easily down my throat. My stomach is getting bigger inside and it's expanding and it feels good in what it now has.'

After this encounter with the imagined good mother there was a distinct improvement in her bearing and she looked at me with a new openness and confidence and altogether she became more animated and no longer so afraid of expressing her emotions.

However, this measure of improvement was still largely confined to her relationship to me and to some extent to her father, but generally speaking she was still what I would call mean with her emotions towards others and she still maintained a degree of secrecy about her personal and artistic interests. She still did not give out much. I had observed earlier that her solar plexus tended to be tight and pulled up, and so I asked her how her stomach felt these days. 'Well,' she said, 'I never really told you this, but I always suffered from stomach cramps and constipation, and I'm still constipated. Also, my periods are still irregular and if I had sex I would be very worried about it. But as it is I'm not worried but it sure feels uncomfortable.' I then decided to investigate her anal retentive syndromes, particularly as they were a natural consequence of her oral retentiveness. I asked her under hypnosis to move forward in time and let her unconscious mind focus upon certain situations which caused her to develop constipation and stomach cramps. I should mention here that I gave up by now using the projection mirror for she could see and experience herself in situations to which we drew attention or as in this case we let her unconscious choose without using the mirror. After a while she saw herself sitting on the potty. 'I feel the rim of it and it's a bit cold. My mother put me on it to do my pooh. My stomach feels full but it would not let it come out. I'm all tense and I want to get away.' I asked her what her bottom and her stomach felt like. 'It's tight and I feel uncomfortable, I have a pain. I won't let it come out because I hate her, I don't want to do it for her. I want to get rid of it but I can't. It feels frightening now. I feel cold and strange. I don't feel secure. I can see my mother now looking at me and she scowls and is unfriendly. She does not like my pooh, she makes me angry. She says I can sit there forever if I like, but I won't move away until I've done it, and she walks out. I feel stubborn, it's a battle. I don't want to let it out to please her, but I must because it hurts. So I push it out and it hurts when I do it but afterwards I feel a bit better, but I'm not happy. I look at my pooh now and it's all mine, it's come out of me, but she does not want it and I won't do what she says. I feel that my stomach is all agitated now and cramped up.' I then ask her like I did earlier in relation to her oral anger to tell me how she would really, deep down in her innermost self want mother to be when she does her pooh. She brightens up visibly: 'I want her to be pleased with what I have done, to smile and be really grateful and I can trust her to like what comes out of me. And then I feel good and (after trying to find the right word) generous.' I then ask her what her stomach and bottom feel like when she is angry. 'My stomach is in a knot and my bottom is tight.' And then I asked her what her stomach and bottom feel like when she feels good in herself and generous and mother is happy with her. 'Oh, ooh, I can feel my stomach opening up, it's not in a knot, it feels good inside there and I can feel my bottom loosening up. Very good. A pleasant sensation. I can trust with it.'

Having established a precedence for this 'generous' feeling we have set a pattern in her mind when her ego could see the possibility of being trustful and generous. It now remained to be seen whether her attitude towards her mother would change or whether she could transfer her good feelings to other female figures and indeed would be able to share her artistic interests. In fact we opened up venues of sublimation, an easing of her stubbornness which facilitate the flow of her libido towards gratification which she could share with others.

I saw this patient for a period of six months, she was sixteen by then, and her relationship with her father had become more confident and trusting and her constipation as well as her stomach cramps had disappeared. Her periods had become more regular and she began to enjoy food and had put on weight. She was still indifferent towards her mother and would react somewhat tetchily to criticism, being what her parents called 'a little temperamental and self-righteous'. I felt confident about her continued improvement, particularly as her sublimatory capacity had greatly improved, and that she would find her identity in the world and be responsive to new challenges and opportunities. I did not question her about her sexual feelings and relationship to boys, but assumed that as her sadistic ties to her father had greatly diminished, her sexual interest would turn towards new relationships. Some two years later a friend of hers told me that she now goes to ballet classes and enjoys them and that she is all right.

There are many variations of the oral experiences during infancy and early childhood and the way individuals respond to them. In our work we come across many persons who have remained fixated upon the oral disturbances which continue to dominate the later stages in the development of their libido, so that for instance as in the just reported case oral-cannibalistic drives dominate their fantasies of the penis, which in turn inhibits the oral-incorporation processes and the receptiveness of the stomach. In other women the oral-aggressive urges are transferred to the vagina which produce sensations of teeth there – 'vagina dentata' – which makes them convinced that men are afraid of them and reject them sexually. This can also lead to an over-emphasis on their clitoris as an aggressive and assertive phallic weapon which can produce painful sensations in this organ. Such fixations upon the early stages of their development will usually remain entirely unconscious while they produce various forms of psychosomatic, neurotic and even psychotic symptoms as well as character disturbances. We only see the outward manifestations of these fixations, the last link in a chain of complex interactions.

Freud has described the problem presented by the persistent psychic fixations both in the aetiology of neurosis and also in the therapeutic process in a very graphic manner, and I take the liberty of quoting him at length. In his essay *Analysis terminable and interminable* he recalls the shrewd satirist of Old Austria, Johann Nestroy, who once said that every advance is only half as great as it looks at first glance: 'One is tempted to think that this malicious dictum is universally valid. There are almost always vestiges of what has been and a partial arrest at a former stage. When an open-handed Maecenas surprises us by some isolated trait of miserliness or a person whose kind-heartedness has been excessive suddenly indulges in some unfriendly act, these are 'vestiges' and are of priceless value for genetic research. They show that these praiseworthy and valuable qualities are based on compensation and over-compensation which, as was only to be expected, have not been absolutely and completely successful. Our first account of libidinal development was that an original oral phase was succeeded by a sadistic-anal, and this in its turn by a phallic-genital phase. Later investigation has not contradicted this view, but we must now qualify our statement by saying that the one phase does not succeed the other suddenly but gradually, so that part of the earlier organization always persists side by side with the later, and that even in normal development the transformation is never complete, the final structure often containing vestiges of earlier libidinal fixations. We see the same thing in quite different connections. There is not one of the erroneous and superstitious beliefs of mankind that are supposed to have been superseded but has left vestiges at the present day in the lower strata of civilised peoples or even in the highest strata of cultivated society. All that has once lived clings tenaciously to life. Sometimes one feels inclined to doubt whether the dragons of primaeval ages are really extinct.'*

There is no doubt that the dragons of primaeval ages continue to exercise their power over man's mind, as we can see in the eruption of sadistic and destructive drives in the behaviour of nations, and we can see it also in the psyche of individuals. The dragons continue to dominate the unconscious mind of otherwise decent and peaceful individuals, not to speak of the brutality and violence among an increasing number of individuals in the 'enlightened and peaceful' societies of the western world.

To illustrate this paradox I shall describe another case where oral-aggressive fixations caused havoc in the personality of a charming and sensitive young woman. I have spoken earlier of this patient, who when looking at the

---

* Sigmund Freud *Collected Papers Vol V* p330

projection mirror saw a frightening monster and after a while discovered that it was her father. She is a fine amateur actress, highly sensitive and intelligent, but was plagued by depression and anxiety states. In her various jobs involved in theatrical production she regularly developed intense but very disturbed relationships with her bosses, became extremely dependent upon them, over-exercised herself to please them, but felt she could never do enough in order to gain their approval. In fact in these matters she was quite paranoiac. Despite her charm, she seemed sexually immature, shy and inhibited. She was overweight and awkward in her movements. She 'naturally' as she put it, could not make proper relationships with men, considering her lack of 'feminine allure'. The only close relationships she could sustain were with homosexual men, but this too was fraught with frustrations and conflicts. She constantly accused them of a lack of devotion and found endless reasons for not being able to trust them. After a while I asked her why she always entered into relationships with homosexuals, and she said, with considerable embarrassment, that she could not trust men. When I persisted and asked what she could not trust them with, she blushed and said that a real man would impale her with his penis. She admitted gradually that she always had the feeling of being a victim and quite helpless about doing anything about it, accompanied by fits of anger which deeply depressed her and proved to herself that she was no good and quite unlovable. We spoke at length about her relationship with her father and how he was betrayed by his partners and lost his business. He became an angry and helpless man and she somehow could feel his anger and could no longer admire him. But he was initially her model of strength and of confidence until he lost his business which was everything to him, and her own self-image turned into one of a disappointed and disappointing person. Like her father she felt she was a failure and became aware of her outrage and anger with him and with herself. In fact, her tantrum-like outbursts of rage were based upon the feeling that she was helpless and couldn't do anything about anything. Indeed tantrums, particularly as they occur in children, are an expression of an aggressive urge that knows that it is unable to make any kind of impact or to further its purposes, and therefore has to be enacted out against the self in a kind of convulsion. While a number of sessions were devoted to the airing of these disturbances, she did not produce significant improvement, they continued to be dominated by this circle of a helpless inability to change anything. We might mention here that the rage-helplessness cycle has many functional characteristics that are similar to manic-depressive cycles.

We decided to go deeper. Under hypnosis I asked her to go back to situations which could be the origins of her helpless tantrums, preceding the trauma of her father's bankruptcy and loss of confidence.

She's five years old in school. She's frightened and insecure, she mistrusts the teacher and is afraid of the other children: 'Mother is not there, I'm frightened of being on my own. I hate being in school away from my parents. I'm isolated and don't have any relationships and no friends, the teacher does not like me.'

I asked her to go back home and who was taking her.

'Auntie takes me home. I go into the house, the hallway is dark, mummy is not there and daddy's always out. Auntie is leaving now and she says mummy is coming soon, I don't know what to do, I feel frightened and I just wait. I hang onto myself. I am quite rigid, it's a long time before mummy comes back. But then she is busy about the house. On Friday night we are all together (it's a Jewish family) but father is not close enough to mummy, they don't hug each other and they don't hug me either. They seem to take no notice of each other. Mother and father are always out together at work and at home there is always this impersonal feeling. I'm not relating to anything, I'm blocked, tight. I'm not hugged. It's not a happy family. Father is a big powerful man, rushing about getting things done, he likes me.'

'Look at him and see how he looks at you.'

'He looks at me lovingly, he likes me but he keeps his distance. He feels my emotions and I want him to hug me and feel his strength, but he rarely does it, he does not show his feelings to me.'

She then spontaneously reflected about her present condition.

'When father lost his business he was no longer a powerful confident man. He was disgusted, I could see this and it made me terribly insecure, everything is dark now, dark.' (Visual manifestation of depressive helplessness.) 'I never became a woman, just a child with a period. I just ran away from men. I'm a woman who is condemned to be a child. My vagina is clamouring, is passionate and furious. It wants to eat. I want to bite the penis off.'

Here we encounter once again the angry vagina occasioned by the loved father who kept himself distant. I asked her in a subsequent session to look at herself in a mirror and observe how she unconsciously sees herself. After some hesitation and signs of horror, she saw herself tight and ungainly with a very frumpish sort of dress. But then she lifted her skirt and saw herself with a great angry vulva with sharp things sticking out. She implored me to stop this, but I refused reassuringly and told her to look carefully. She now saw herself naked, with teeth in her vagina which hurt, and also a snarling biting expression in her face. I ask: 'Why do the teeth in the vagina hurt?'

'I can feel they want to bite the penis and it would hurt him. I can feel the hurt. I'm a nasty person, men get angry with me, they want to revenge themselves on me, I want them to revenge themselves on me, to destroy me, to break my teeth, to castrate me, but it's frightening. I have to be nice to placate them, reassure them, so they can't see or feel my teeth. So I eat a lot to satisfy my hunger and cover up my ferocity and to be nice and fat and harmless. But then nothing happens, my vagina is still ferocious and I have to hide it. I pretend I don't feel it, I pretend it does not exist. Do I really exist? I'm just pretending to be nice and do things for men, but they know better, they don't trust me, they want other women. Everything I do is no good. So I hate everything and everything hates me. Do you call this paranoia? So then I'm paranoiac. I want to get out of this. I want to be alluring and attractive and assertive and show that I want men and make them want me but with my figure that's hopeless.'

I pointed out that all she is doing is hiding her ferocity, so let's get in touch with this ferocity and find out how it originated.

We then took her back to being a baby without much difficulty: 'The nipple is hard, it's embarrassed and alien. I'm worried about the nipple, it may come off. I don't know how to take it, it feels strange, my lips don't feel its shape, I don't know how to shape my lips around it. Nothing happens, I don't ever expect anything to happen. I'm becoming quite desperate. I'm trying to suck, I'm sucking hard but nothing comes out. I bite to make something happen, I feel it now but mummy is frightened. But I like the biting and I want mummy to react even if she is frightened. But then I like the angry feeling. Her fear makes me feel I am angry. That's the only way to get something. But then mummy pushes me and goes away. She is frightened of all these feelings and just wants to finish it as quickly as possible and get away. She's no longer thinking about me. She does not really get any pleasure from daddy so she does not get any pleasure from me. I'm just a nuisance, she's impatient, I prevent her from doing business with daddy. She's a business woman, all matter-of-fact, but she's dissatisfied. No warmth there.'

I have found that if patients can translate their infantile sensations of the mother into grown-up words, they show an astonishing empathy which may be almost telepathic with her feelings and her states of mind. It is possible to encourage them to do this either by having them ask mother what is the matter with her and what's in her mind, or to tell me direct what their impression of mother's state of mind is. Sometimes these insights have a powerful impact upon the patient's ego and by understanding mother's motivations they feel they can almost forgive her; they achieve a measure of dominance and cease to feel helpless victims of an incomprehensible fate. When I then asked this patient to feel and see what she really wanted her mother to be like and how she really wanted to feel her, she responded with what I have learned to be an almost instinctual response, expressing the 'natural' innate urges for pleasurable satisfaction, for a happy mother who feels pleasure in giving herself to the baby and enjoys the baby's pleasure. She said that now her vagina also feels it and wants to open up and suck and feel the happy penis which has pleasure with her. It can now show itself. It is no longer ferocious with hunger and she knows now that it is good and that what she wants is good. She later told me that she no longer has to stuff food with a kind of helpless greed but can now enjoy eating and that her stomach feels good when she eats. And she is pleased with the feeling in her stomach. And this, with some expression of astonishment, she said also meant that she feels good with her whole body. Indeed, she became slimmer and a more 'pleasantly cheeky' and seductive woman.

9 The Treatment of Psychotic Patients

1. EGO LOSS AND INFANTILISM

A number of psychoanalysts have attempted to find a way of treating psychotic patients. Although some of these attempts have yielded illuminating insights into the nature of this baffling condition, the therapeutic results have remained largely disappointing. Indeed, it is generally accepted that psychotics are intractable to psychological treatment. One of the reasons for the near impossibility of making much therapeutic headway, or even of making any meaningful contact with such individuals, lies in the weakness or even absence of their ego functions, so that a therapist cannot relate to these patients in any rational manner. Whatever another person, including a psychiatrist or a psychotherapist, may say to a psychotic will remain entirely irrelevant and unreal.

I had a psychotic patient who 'knew' that the devil was speaking to him and had told him that noises emanating from machines would enter his brain and destroy it. He therefore spent much of his time clutching his ears, pretending not to hear anything in order to ward off those mind-destroying noises. Curiously enough, when he was sent to me he was interested in what I might say, as he thought I could explain what these machines were trying to do to him, and thought of me as a helpful representative of the devil. He therefore took me to be his friend, and was prepared to listen to me. I had established an emotional contact and a measure of transference on the basis of becoming part of his delusion. We spent a few sessions talking about various aspects of his life history and the nature of his delusional world. As our communication remained circular – confined within the bubble of his delusions – I made an attempt to break through his delusions. I put it to him that as an intelligent person he must know that there was no devil in heaven (he thought that the devil occupied the heavens and spoke to him from there.) He looked at me with wide-eyed astonishment and considerable disappointment and said that he thought that I was an intelligent person who knew about the devil and he was very disappointed by my lack of understanding. There was no way of making any realistic contact with him, that is, outside his own view of things. Such individuals will either regard you as a fool or simply not take any notice of what you think or what you have to say. You represent a dimension of existence which is absent to them, namely their ego function, and they have, therefore, no way of recognising another person's ego functions. What particularly interests me, however, is the question of how they have lost this dimension of the psyche, because I assume that they were not born with this incapacity. It is easy enough to recognise that their ego is severely impaired or even absent, but the question for me is what they have done with it, what their psyche has done to destroy it. One can say that they have been arrested at the pre-ego stage of their development and are therefore dominated by infantile psychic processes. But again, why should this be the case? In my work it has become clear that whatever psychic disorders and symptoms afflict an individual, they are the product of his own psychic activity; every patient produces his own conflicts and symptoms. This has become the cornerstone of my understanding of psychic processes and of the therapy I have pursued. Of course, with a neurotic person we have an agreement that there is something wrong with him, that he suffers from a debility which impairs his proper functioning and causes him considerable suffering and that he wants us to help him to regain his health. A psychotic, on the other hand, considers that his hallucinations reflect a real state of affairs and his bizarre behaviour is normal or inevitable. This sense of inevitability precludes any kind of dialectic between illness and health and therefore intervention, from the point of view of what we consider normality and realism, is impossible. Frieda Fromm-Reichmann, who was one of the pioneers in the psychoanalytic treatment of schizophrenia, often said that the first thing to do in the treatment of such cases is to establish a bridge of understanding between patient and therapist, to look for an area of agreement from which one can judge the patient's illness. This applies to all psychotic syndromes, including manic-depressive cycles, ambulatory mania, paranoia, schizophrenia, catatonia, mental disassociation and bizarre behaviour patterns. It is perfectly correct to say that the establishment of such a bridge between the ego of the therapist and the ego of the patient is essential, but in many, even most, cases of psychosis it is impossible to do this. A psychotic may agree with what you have to say to him but will remain emotionally entirely untouched, or, on the other hand, as I have said, he will completely dismiss as irrelevant or silly whatever you try to say or explain to him.

I found, however, that many of these patients are able to enter into hypnotic states. The above-mentioned patient readily agreed to be hypnotised and proved to be an excellent subject. At first I avoided confrontation with his unconscious ego in the mirror, for I assumed that this would be too painful and frightening for him, and we initiated age regression. He returned to completely forgotten events in his early childhood. He had lost all memory of his mother, claiming that he had never known her. He was, however, told that his mother was a prostitute, and he was brought up by his grandparents. Under hypnosis he readily told me his life history.

He saw himself with his grandparents whom he liked, but they couldn't really look after him because they were rather frail and he was too much of a burden on them. When he was five he was taken to a home, at twelve he absconded and came to London, where he survived as a boy prostitute, became involved in crime and drug-trafficking, and spent much of his time in remand homes, mental hospitals and, later, in prisons. He could not at first remember at what age he came under the influence of the devil, but by the time he was sixteen he started to be obsessed with the fear of sounds coming from machines, and began to cover his ears in order to avoid them. I asked him how he could hear his friend the devil speaking to him when he covered his ears. He laughed at me, again amazed at my silliness, and said that of course he could hear the devil, when all he had to do was to keep out those noises, because, quite reasonably, the devil asked him to do this. He had various forms of drug therapy which made him, as he said, lose his mind, and, although he was then less frightened of the sounds, he could not think at all and felt like a zombie and even had difficulty in communicating with the devil. He was then released, but shortly after his release his hallucinations and motor obsessions returned.

Upon taking him back to infancy, to about six months old, under hypnosis, he saw his mother. She held him gently but at a kind of distance, as if he did not belong to her. She seemed to be overwhelmed with a sorrow, and he felt it: 'She was always lying in bed, and with different men.' He met his father, who was a client of his mother, and described them both vividly and with much feeling. He liked his father, who had shown affection to the boy, and remembered him ringing the bell whenever he came to visit. But one day his father again rang the bell and told his mother that he was taking her away with him and that she had to take the child to live with his grandparents. She took him to the grandparents and then she was gone. His father, whom he came to love, visited him a few times at his grandparents, but whenever he rang the bell the boy got into a state of terror, for it meant that he would take mother away or rather, it reminded him that he was taking mother away, and he put his hands around his ears. I asked him to describe the sound emanating from the machine, and it was indeed the ringing sound of a bell. And the bell was a machine that announced the disappearance of his mother. He did not want to live without his mother, he did not, as he put it, 'want to exist'. Whatever would happen from now on had nothing to do with him. His father was the omnipotent devil whom he had loved but who also announced that his mother would cease to exist for him. He had destroyed the boy's emotional attachment, his link to his mother, and killed his feelings from then on, and he sort of lived beside himself, and whatever happened had nothing really to do with him. We see here the destruction of the internal object, the negation of the sense of self which depended upon the internalised sensations and images of his mother, and when this was denied the child's ego felt denied, destroyed, and a sense of vacuum appeared in his soul. We can speak here of a self-destruction of the ego in a tantrum of rage which turns against the self denied. I have found again and again in psychotic patients that it is in fact the destruction of the internal object which profoundly weakens or eliminates the narcissistic ego and hence eliminates the sense of ego relationship to the objective, real world.

When he was sixteen the patient was told that his mother had died, and it was then that the memory of the ringing machine – the bell – overwhelmed him, and he became preoccupied with the obsession of having to elude this sound, for it reminded him of the disappearance of his mother and the death of his libido. He had previously transferred much of his affection to his father, and he became the only link with life; he loved him but he also was the announcer, the messenger of the death of his soul.

This is a very abridged record of the many experiences

which had been uncovered, mostly during hypnosis, but it illustrates the process which had led to the undoing of an intolerable reality and of his ego functions. With the return of these memories, vividly re-experienced, a sense of self began to establish itself in this patient, and he could speak of himself as 'I' and relate to the real world. He eventually took a job looking after dogs in a kennel, and frequently came to visit me after his treatment was finished. Indeed, he was keen for me to show him to my colleagues as an example of successful treatment, which I refused. He obviously wanted to rehabilitate himself in the eyes of his psychiatrists who always saw him as a madman.

This case happened many years ago and was one of the first in my experiences which showed me the possibility of curing psychotics by psychological means.

The process by which a person denies the ego functions, indeed destroys them, is perhaps even better illustrated by the treatment of another patient.

2. THE GOOD-BAD CONUNDRUM

I have earlier spoken of the patient who repelled all her husband's approaches with considerable ferocity and would not allow him to touch her. I was able to establish a good rapport with her and our conversations came easily and naturally. Only when I implied that an erotic relationship with her husband would be a source of gratification and pleasure between them did she show signs of anger and resentment, and usually managed to change the subject. She often spoke of her sense of estrangement from her home where she felt an outsider and unwanted, of her feeling that she was not really part of her family and frequently had bouts of jealousy and resentment towards her children. She admitted that she usually felt morose and unloving, hated going to bed with her husband, did not really want to cook or do the usual tasks connected with being a wife and mother. Their evening meals were taken in an atmosphere of cold resentment, and all she could think of was how to delay having to go to the bedroom. As I mentioned earlier, she was an exceptionally well-dressed and elegant woman, with good taste for style and colour. One of the criticisms she used to make of her husband was his lack of care for his appearance and particularly the state of his dressing-gown, which made her feel disgusted, and the uncouth way he was usually dressed at home. I may mention that he is a tall, good-looking man, well-dressed at work and on his visits to me. When I spoke to him about his wife's criticism, he was baffled, but admitted that he likes to take it easy and feel comfortable when at home. I mention these matters here because they turned out to be relevant in the subsequent analysis. While she felt generally unreal, ill at ease and resentful at home and liked to go out shopping, her visits to shops became a nightmare; she was filled with anxiety and confusion, and even though she managed to buy some good clothes, these expeditions were a source of acute anxiety, till she was unable to continue them.

We could have gone on forever talking about these matters, and no doubt in classic analysis one could have done so, but they did not lead to any particular insights and covered up some deep-seated fears, which she was determined to keep repressed. Above all, she refused to acknowledge that her behaviour and her attitudes towards her husband and children were in any way unnatural or abnormal. She did not consider them as symptomatic of some kind of disturbance but defended them as perfectly natural and inevitable. All this after four years of psychoanalysis in which almost every session ended in a state of anxiety and confusion! When she drove home from her session she was in a state of panic and confusion and frequently lost her way driving around London, not knowing where she was or what she was doing. However, she usually did manage to get home. While she did not consider herself to be neurotic or mentally disturbed, she admitted that she was very unhappy.

We agreed to find out the deeper causes for her unhappiness and, for this purpose, to hypnotise her. In the body analysis she became aware of a tight chest, uneasy and somewhat painful feelings in her stomach, and tight legs. I refrained from conducting her body analysis in any great depth, because I did not want to arouse sexual feelings which would have caused her great anxiety, with a likelihood of developing a negative transference with profound fear and hostility towards me, which would probably have caused her to withdraw from analysis. In the mirror she saw herself hunched up in a corner, with a hollow chest, drawn in shoulders and altogether rigid with fear. Above all, she appeared to be hiding herself. We obviously dealt with acute sexual anxiety and a narcissistic injury, a narcissistic shrinking process. After a couple of sessions in which we explored her defensive and mistrustful attitude to men, her sense of isolation at home and, in particular, in society, which she recalled also in her childhood, she spontaneously went back to a situation at the age of two-and-a-half which proved to be decisive for her development. She was in bed with her father, and clearly and easily spoke of the nice and pleasant feeling of closeness with him. She then hesitated, as if she experienced a new sensation. She felt her father's penis, and it was nice and warm, and she felt her father's pleasure. She held it in her hand, and then he gave a sigh and she felt a wetness in her hand. He had ejaculated, and the little girl liked her father and she felt close to him and was not in the least disturbed. But then all of a sudden her mother came into the room. Her father went rigid with fear, her mother saw what had happened and started to scream and went mad with fury and outrage. She went berserk and absolutely terrified the child. The child knew then that she had done something terrible and caused her father to do some terrible thing which so outraged the mother. It seemed that the mother became hysterical, and the child was frightened and equally hysterical with fear. She should not have done it, she did not want it to have happened. She ran to a corner in the room and faced the wall and went rigid. She stared at the wall and pretended she no longer existed. She recalled vividly how, by staring at the wall, she immobilised herself, all awareness of what she had done and all awareness of the world disappeared. She in fact negated herself in order to eradicate this terrible thing which had so outraged her mother. One can say that she attempted to induce a catatonic state in herself, for what constitutes catatonia is a state of mental and sensory immobility, where the perception of time and space is all but eliminated and, above all, all the ego functions cease to operate. In other words, it is a condition of mental deadness, even while fundamental physiological functions continue to operate. This girl, however, did not succeed in inducing catatonia, nor did her negation of her sense of self continue for long. Her mother jerked her out of the room and told her in no uncertain terms to get on with whatever she had to do, while she went to berate her husband. However, the state of mind, which the girl attempted to induce, continued to persist in certain areas of her psyche as a negative reaction formation against the pursuit of pleasurable satisfactions of any kind: a profound taboo against her desire to please, a contraction and near elimination of the narcissistic libido, and particularly a taboo upon sexual feelings. She thought of herself as a seductress who had aroused her father and brought humiliation, shame and punishment upon him, and she continued to be a danger to men. What she had thought to be her good feelings were in fact bad, a danger to men, and she had to rebuff their erotic advances in order to protect them from herself. She had loved her father and did not think that he had done anything wrong; he was just loving and, being frustrated by a vindictive and unloving mother, turned to her for a little love and gratification. But it was her fault for having loved him and touched him and led him on and arousing the terrible rage of her mother.

Her fear of leading men on and arousing their sexual desires and, with it, her sense of self-condemnation, was reinforced years later, when she was about ten years old.

She and a girlfriend were playing near a railway line (her father was a railway man) when a man in a railway man's uniform approached the girls and started to chat with them. Her girlfriend ran away but she did not feel any need to do so, for he was after all a railway man like her father (by that time she had forgotten her earlier trauma.) She chatted with him in a friendly way. But then he tried to fondle her. She then got into a panic and ran away. When she got home she was distraught but did not tell her mother what had happened. However, the other girl soon told the mother about the railway man approaching them, and she again became hysterical with fury, and a scene which was similar to that which happened years ago repeated itself. The girl this time did not repeat her attempt at catatonia, but became withdrawn, overwhelmed by guilt feelings and convinced that she was bad. For after all, the other girl did the sensible thing and ran away, while she stayed with the railway man and led him on to becoming sexually excited; she had practically seduced him. It was once again her fault, and she was an undeniably bad girl, rejected and condemned, not only by her mother but by the whole world. She was condemned by the superego, the omnipotent judge, the all-seeing eye, so that her ego, her self, had no right to exist. The first trauma repeated itself here, but was not experienced on such an all-encompassing level; it did not repeat the catatonic negation of the ego functions but produced a split in the ego. On the one hand, she was sympathetic and understanding towards her father, and he presented her with a good breast/penis, and had overcome the negative, unloving experience of her mother/breast. She introjected the good feel of her father and identified with him in a sympathetic empathy, but, on the other hand, her mother attacked the introjected father and her ego identity with him, and made what was good, bad, what was loving, disgusting and unacceptable. This time the good identification did not disappear but became a source of guilt and anxiety and had to be hidden as the secret self. Her attraction and sympathy towards males became the secret shame of being a seductress, and at the same time the ability to seduce expressed itself as a preconscious desexualised pleasure in being attractive. In being attractive she preserved the good libido, which, at the same time, isolated her from the world as being an expression of her badness. When she was eleven her father died, and as her mother was by then a paranoid, hysterical woman who could not cope with a young daughter, she was sent to a children's home. Under hypnosis, she recalled in great detail her agony at having her clothes taken away and having to wear institutional clothing. She felt that her identity was now finally obliterated, that she was punished for trying to hold on to a part of herself which she could call her own, that it was taken away from her and she was not allowed to be herself. She spoke with great passion about her outrage and pain and of the many periods during her stay in this home when she suffered from mental dissociation and confusion when everything felt unreal. She could not accept or comprehend the rules which dominated the children's lives and was intensely aware of the animosity of the matron who punished and frightened her. She once again felt lost and rejected. When I got her to look at herself in the mirror at that age, she saw the angry expression of the matron which turned into a picture of her mother as a monstrous, hysterical being. After a while she saw herself hiding herself in a corner and wanting to disappear. We can recognise that her clothes represented her narcissistic sense of identity, and when they were taken away she once again disappeared, only aware of the rage of the maternal superego.

After about three years she left the children's home to live with relatives, and gradually regained her narcissistic ego functions. But she continued to feel unreal in the world, an outsider, a fundamentally bad woman, and while she never felt at home anywhere, she desexualised herself during puberty and after. While she managed to recreate her image of an attractive woman, which, to some extent, saved her sanity, it was nevertheless a symbol of being a seductress, and, as such, made her an outcast and rejected by the world, nowhere at home and belonging nowhere. She eventually got married, but she felt a sense of unreality in her home, could not perceive or feel herself as a wife or mother, was constantly plagued by anxieties and paranoid delusions, and was particularly concerned with resenting her husband's erotic feelings, for they reminded her of her bad self and provoked her feeling of being a seductress. She had to rebuff her husband, often in quite violent terms, in order to protect herself and also to protect him from her secret self. It is interesting in this connection to note that before they were married she could submit sexually, albeit without any sexual feelings, and it was one of the corner-stones of her treatment when she remembered that when she met his family she wanted desperately to be accepted by them, but suddenly, on the first day of being married, she had a vision that they all resented and hated her. From then on she could not allow herself to yield to him, and had to show that she was not going to harm him with her seductive powers, which were the cause of all her troubles.

As we uncovered the traumas which made her, in many respects but not entirely, psychotic, we gradually enabled her to accept the good sides of her sexual self, making her feel that she belonged in her home, and that it was hers. Beyond that, we enabled her to enjoy the beauty of nature, to open her eyes to the erotic symbolism of flowers, colours and designs, and enjoy them without guilt. She began to paint and write poetry, and came to accept her husband's desires, as she could accept her own. It is significant that with the reinstatement of her genital libido and, in particular, her narcissistic libido, she came to feel herself a real person and accepted by and accepting the world around her.

I have described this case in some detail for it illustrates the process of ego destruction, and then, later, the intense conflict between the good and the bad libido, leading to her self negation and to the negation of sexuality. Of course every single case is different, and the way psychotic disturbances originate varies enormously, but they all have in common a deep narcissistic injury, sustained at an early age, often at about two years old. The loss of the ego functions produces a regression to an infantile, pre-ego reaction formation, which comes to dominate the psyche, in some cases completely, in others almost completely.

3. THE PROSPECT OF TREATING HOSPITALISED PSYCHOTICS

The treatment of the two patients I have described above illustrates the possibility not only of curing psychosis by psychological means but also of gaining new insights into the nature of this complex and baffling disease. While I have treated these cases and others of a similar nature in private practice, the large majority of psychotics are only accessible in mental hospitals or, more recently, in clinics and hostels. The question which thus forces itself upon one is whether it is possible to arrive at a treatment method which can be applied in the hospital environment. The desirability of such treatment, if it could be shown to be successful, is self-evident; the problems of drug therapy are well attested, and we see the failures not only inside the hospitals but also in the streets of big cities. The social cost of hospitalisation, as well as of the wasted lives of tens of thousands of individuals, is a considerable burden upon society, but beyond that we are increasingly made aware of the tragedies of such ruined lives.

Can we, therefore, learn something from the treatment which I have undertaken with psychotics, and can we apply these lessons to the hospital environment? The successes which I have been able to achieve with some patients in this category embolden me to think that the methods I have adopted could be equally used, with certain modifications but essentially based upon the same principles, in hospitals or clinics. The first question we have to consider is whether the majority of psychotics would be amenable to hypnosis, and whether they even consider it necessary to 'cure' them of their mental disease. The two patients I have described did not present any particular difficulty, in fact they readily accepted hypnosis, not so much because they thought there was anything wrong with their minds, but because they were frequently frightened and unhappy.

But before I discuss the most suitable methods of hypnotic induction for psychotics in the hospital environment, I want to draw attention once again to the element of empathy with the patient's disorder. This is of particular significance in the treatment of psychotics, for we deal here, more so than in neurotic patients, with the infantile level of emotional expression. The psychological treatment of psychotics is largely concerned with psychic processes which are incomprehensible to the perception and judgements of the observer. In order to 'understand' or get the feel of the meaning of their behaviour or fantasies, the therapist has to have some knowledge of the pre-verbal experiences of the small child, and at the same time some emotional contact with the infantile processes which dominate the patient. He has to be sufficiently unrepressed towards his own infantile emotions to recognise their meaning when he observes them in the psychotic. It is therefore desirable that the therapist is in contact with his own infantile feelings at least to some extent, in order to enable him to understand patients.

For example: we may be called upon to treat a patient who throws himself about, often quite violently, either accompanied by screams or quietly. What is he doing? He is displaying emotional expression on a pre-ego, pre-verbal level, he is obsessed by the need to give vent to his fears, rages, anxieties, in an infantile form of behaviour. Indeed, we can see a grown-up individual enacting an infantile tantrum. But whereas the child's tantrum recedes after a while, the grown-up, who has regressed to a stage of childhood or infancy, has no hope of achieving any response from his environment or obtaining any gratification from his behaviour, and therefore is frozen in his tantrum, and has to go on till he is physically exhausted. And the energy available to such patients is usually quite astonishing, and reminds one of the energy available to a hypnotised person; indeed, it would not be far wrong to speak here of an auto-hypnotic form of regression. The child's tantrum is usually a form of emotional communication in a state of helplessness, unable to anticipate a response, attention or reward by other means. If the child does not anticipate that its call for attention will be responded to, it gives up its capacity for verbal communication and regresses to infantile, somatic forms of expression. The psychotic has eliminated his ego functions and is dominated by infantile modes of communication.

Psychiatrists are acquainted with a wide range of violent self-torturing or apparently harmless, obsessive patterns of behaviour. I have seen some women who ceaselessly open and close their legs, grimacing, laughing and crying at the same time, often accompanied by actions which clearly express rejection or warding-off gestures. With such cases a sexual element is unmistakable, and they hysterically enact sexual urges as well as taboos at the same time, and it all leads nowhere. They are trapped in a conflict which they once acted out as children but which could not find a sublimated form of expression. Desire and rejection are enacted in a somatic drama which has become a self-perpetuating reflex. Tics have been analysed as a conflict between turning towards an object of desire and its negation. In a psychotic individual such a tic represents an all-encompassing conflict which absorbs the whole psyche, and there is no room for the ego to do anything or think about anything else. We must remember however that thinking is carried out on a somatic level, as I have observed earlier.

Psychopathic behaviour, on the other hand, does relate to other persons, who represent a primary object which has aroused the child's rage and aggression. Psychopaths transfer their infantile rage upon the grown-up world but have repressed the primary situation which gave rein to their anger. The child's aggressive drive is re-enacted ad infinitum in a state of unconscious transference to the world of grown-ups. They are frozen in this rage which can never find reward and therefore appears meaningless. It is the very meaninglessness of their behaviour which makes it obsessive.

From a psychoanalytic view, every individual dominated by manic fantasies has killed the superego and taken on its role. The constraints of the ego are eliminated, the ego boundaries dissolved. In order to exist at all he has to be omnipotent. But having killed the father figure in his mind, and taken the place of the infantile image of the father as the all-powerful giant, he is then visited by remorse, and retreats into mourning, being punished and having to suffer for his deed. In every case of mania we can see an acting out of the Oedipus complex without the constraints of the ego and the reality principle. I should mention that of course intense physiological and chemical changes accompany these states, but they are in response to all-pervading psychological drives and fuel their purpose, so to speak.

The compulsions of defiance and punishment, the gestures of warding-off and rejection of aggressive or sexual urges, are countless in their variety and fill psychiatric hospitals. I have mentioned catatonia as the supreme manifestation of rage which turns against the self and obliterates it. If we look at psychotics from the point of view of the child and the logic of the unconscious mind, however bizarre and strange it may appear, we enter into the mind of these patients and may overcome our own repressions, which make us unable to understand them. For one must not underestimate our own defences and hostility when confronted by the demonic forces made manifest by psychotics.

Even so, any 'normal' communication with such individuals is usually very difficult and, even if it were possible, would not lead to a cessation of their pathologies. It is therefore left to the power of hypnosis to reinstate the patients' ego functions by enabling them to re-live the experiences which have given rise to their pathologies. The question, however, arises how the induction of hypnosis would in practice be possible. I have mentioned earlier that I have, as it were, reached an agreement with my patients that it is worthwhile and desirable to enter into the hypnotic or rather, hypnoid state. The two psychotic patients I have described readily agreed and approved of the procedure. I had for various reasons achieved a measure of rapport with them, and they trusted me. But with most psychotics such levels of transference, understanding and agreement could not be expected. With them it would be useful to give the impression of magic, in order to interest them, and this magic could be represented by some machine, namely, a hypnotising machine, with lights flashing and mysterious noises emanating from it. The advantage of this would be that such objects appear impersonal and powerful at the same time, and the transference element, which is so difficult to achieve in a person-to-person relationship, would be displaced from the psychiatrist to a machine. We live in a world where machines, even to the normal person, have become a symbol of omnipotence, and much more so to the infantile mind of a psychotic. Such a procedure would also free the therapist from the strain of having to make contact with the patient, which is often an anxiety-making experience. We can thus sit the patient in front of this magic machine and, after a few reassuring words, let it take over.

There are a number of well-researched techniques to induce a hypnotic state by means of a machine. There is the pendulum with a light at the end of it, or lights flashing rhythmically, or a rotating mirror with a light shining on it, or a fast revolving spiral with colours and lights. These are just some of the techniques one can experiment with. The advantage of these techniques is that they do not have to rely on the interest or curiosity of the patient but use what is called fascination technique or visual confusion, which have the power to disturb the defence mechanism and armour of the patient. After he begins to feel disorientated, which produces tiredness and inability to keep his eyes open, the therapist will induce the hypnotic trance in the classical manner. In those cases I do not attempt to use my usual method of hypnoid induction, which does rely on the patient's co-operation and imaginative ability, but employ hypnosis in considerable depth. One could employ a professional hypnotist to perform induction, and, after he has produced a sufficient degree of hypnotic depth, he could hand over to the therapist, and depth analysis can proceed from there. The methods of depth analysis would be similar to those I have described with other cases. On the body analytic level, gestures and postures, repetitive actions, paralyses and compulsive behaviour patterns could be observed and analysed as to their meaning in the projection mirror. In my experience, the sense of recognition derived from these procedures can be quite startling and intense. The process of regression and re-experience of the unconscious origins of their particular symptoms would be the same as described.

I can foresee no particular difficulty in implementing such procedures in the hospital setting, with the possible exception of violent motor restlessness. In such cases, one could tie the patients to a chair and make them look at the machine, and it would be most likely to have the desired effect. In particularly difficult cases, one could produce a drowsy effect by means of injections, but I do not favour this method, because one wants the patient's mind to be as alert as possible. These procedures would require a number of sessions over a few weeks or months, although some cases would respond quite dramatically in a short space of time. The cost of the treatment would probably be less in the long run than the traditional psychiatric regimen. But besides the likely improvement rate achieved, the contribution to our understanding of the most baffling of all human disturbances would be considerable.

Indeed, it is the psychotic individual who is most deeply rooted in what we call our unconscious mind; he spends his life in a region of the mind which the rest of us have left behind and forgotten, so that we no longer know it exists and have no understanding of it. We may consider that the psychotic inhabits the unknown world of the psyche, and by understanding him we may begin to reclaim that vast continent of our unconscious and be enriched by it.

Bibliography

Abraham, Karl: *A Short Study in the Development of the Libido* (Hogarth Press, 1927)
 − *Selected Papers on Psychoanalysis* (Hogarth Press, 1955)
Adorno, T & Horkheimer, M: *Aspects of Sociology* (London, 1979)
Adorno, T et al: *The Authoritarian Family* (Norton, 1969)
Alexander, Franz: *Psychoanalysis and Psychotherapy* (George Allen & Unwin, 1957)
Balint, Michael: *Primary Love and Psychoanalytic Technique* (Hogarth Press, 1959)
Bernfeld, S: *Psychology of the Infant* (Kegan Paul, 1929)
 − 'Sigmund Freud' in *International Journal of Psychoanalysis 1951*
Bettelheim, Bruno: *The Informed Heart* (Peregrine, 1986)
Bion, W R: 'Attacks on Linking' in *International Journal of Psychoanalysis 1959 Vol 40 pp308-315*
Bornemann, Ernest: *The Psychoanalysis of Money* (Urizen Books, 1976)
Bowlby, J: *Attachment and Loss:*
   Vol. 1 *Attachment* (New Edition, 1982)
   Vol. 2 *Separation, Anxiety and Anger* (1980)
   Vol. 3 *Loss − Sadness and Depression* (1980)
         (Hogarth Press)
Breggin, Peter: *Toxic Psychiatry* (Fontana, 1993)
Breuer, Joseph & Freud, Sigmund: *Studies on Hysteria* (Penguin Freud Library, Vol 3)
Brown, J A C: *Freud and the Post-Freudians* (Pelican, 1961)

BIBLIOGRAPHY

Brown, N O: *Life against Death* (London, 1968)

Chodorow, N: *The Reproduction of Mothering: Psychoanalysis and the Sociology of Gender* (California, 1978)

Deleuze, G & Guattari, F: *Anti-Oedipus: Capitalism and Schizophrenia* (Viking Press, 1977)

Deutsch, Helene: *The Psychology of Female Sexuality* (1925) – *The Psychology of Women, Vol 2* (Grune & Stratton, 1945)

Dubos, R: *So Human an Animal* (Rupert Hart-Davis, 1970)

Ellenberger, H F: *The Discovery of the Unconscious – The History and Evolution of Dynamic Psychiatry* (Allen & Unwin, 1970)

Erikson, E H: *Childhood and Society* (Norton, 1964) – *Identity: Youth and Crisis* (Faber, 1971)

Fairbairn, W R D: *An Object Relations Theory of the Personality* (Basic Books, 1954)

Federn, Paul: *Ego Psychology and the Psychoses* (Basic Books, 1952)

Fenichel, O: *The Psychoanalytic Theory of Neurosis* (Routledge, 1960) – 'A Critique of the Death Instinct' in *Collected Papers* (Norton, 1953)

Ferenczi, S: *Contributions to Psychoanalysis* (Hogarth Press, 1955)

Foucault, M: *The History of Sexuality,* (Pantheon, 1978)

Frankl, George: *The Failure of the Sexual Revolution* (Kahn & Averill, 1974) – *The Social History of the Unconscious* Paperback edition in two volumes: *Vol 1 Archaeology of the Mind* *Vol 2 Civilisation – Utopia and Tragedy* (Open Gate Press, 1989 & 1992) – *The Unknown Self* (Open Gate Press, 1990)

Frankl, Victor: *The Will to Meaning* (Souvenir Press, 1971)

Franz, M-L von: 'The Process of Individuation' in *Man and his Symbols,* edited by C G Jung (1960)

Freud, Anna: *The Ego and the Mechanisms of Defence* (Hogarth Press, 1986)

BIBLIOGRAPHY

Freud, Sigmund: see *The Standard Edition of the Complete Psychological Works of Sigmund Freud* (24 Volumes);
(1900) *The Interpretation of Dreams* (Vols 4-5)
(1905) *Three Essays on the Theory of Sexuality* (Vol 7)
(1908) *Character and Anal Eroticism* (Vol 9)
(1913) *Totem and Taboo* (Vol 13)
(1914) *On Narcissism* (Vol 14)
(1915) *The Unconscious* (Vol 14)
(1915/17) *Introductory Lectures on Psychoanalysis* (Vol 15-16)
(1920) *Beyond the Pleasure Principle* (Vol 18)
(1921) *Group Psychology and the Analysis of the Ego* (Vol 18)
(1923) *The Ego and the Id* (Vol 19)
(1925) *Some Psychical Consequences of the Anatomical Distinction between the Sexes* (Vol 19)
(1927) *The Future of an Illusion* (Vol 21)
(1930) *Civilisation and its Discontents* (Vol 21)
(1933) *New Introductory Lectures on Psychoanalysis* (Vol 22)
(1938) *An Outline of Psychoanalysis* (Vol 23)
Fromm, Erich: *Fear of Freedom* (Routledge, 1960)
– *Psychoanalysis of Religion* (Yale, 1950)
– *The Sane Society* (Routledge Paperback, 1963)
– *The Revolution of Hope* (Harper & Row, 1968)
– *The Crisis of Psychoanalysis* (Holt, Rinehart & Winston, 1970)
– *The Anatomy of Human Destruction* (J Cape, 1974)
Gedo, J & Pollock, G H: *Freud – The Fusion of Science and Humanism* (Psychological Issues, 1975)
Glover, Edward: *Psychoanalysis* (John Bale, 1939)
– *On the Early Development of the Mind* (Unwin, 1956)
– *The Birth of the Ego* (Allen & Unwin, 1968)
Groddeck, Georg: *The Book of the It* (N M D, 1928)
Guntrip, Harry: *Personality Structure and Human Interaction* (Hogarth Press, 1961)
– *Schizoid Phenomena, Object Relations and the Self* (Hogarth Press, 1968)

Hartmann, H: *Ego Psychology and the Problem of Adaptation* (International Universities Press, 1958)

Haynal, André: *Psychoanalysis and the Sciences* (Karnac Books, 1992)

Horkheimer, Max: *Autorität und Familie* (Paris, 1936)

Jahoda, M: *Freud and the Dilemma of Psychology* (Hogarth Press, 1977)

Jones, Ernest: *The Life and Work of Sigmund Freud* (Hogarth Press, 1957)

Jung, C G: *Symbols of Transformation* (Routledge, 1956)
- *On the Psychology of the Unconscious* (London, 1952)
- *Modern Man in Search of his Soul* (London, 1953)

Kinsey, A et al: *Sexual Behaviour in the Human Female* (W B Saunders & Company, 1953)

Klein, Melanie: *Contributions to Psychoanalysis* (Hogarth Press, 1948)
- *The Psychoanalysis of Children* (Hogarth Press, 1932)
- *Envy and Gratitude* (Tavistock, 1957)

Klein, M et al: *Developments in Psychoanalysis* (Hogarth Press, 1952)

Koestler, Arthur: *The Ghost in the Machine* (Hutchinson, 1967)

Koestler, A et al: *The God that Failed* (London, 1950)

Kohut, H: *The Analysis of the Self* (International Universities Press, 1971)

Lacan, Jacques: 'The Function and Field of Speech and Language in Psychoanalysis' in *Ecrits* (English transl. London, 1977)

Laing, R D: *The Divided Self* (Penguin, 1960)

Langs, Robert: *Science, Systems, and Psychoanalysis* (Karnac Books, 1992)

Laplanche, Jean: *New Foundations for Psychoanalysis* (Warner Books, 1979)

Laplanche, J & Pontalis, J B: *The Language of Psychoanalysis* (Hogarth Press, 1973)

Lash, Christopher: *The Culture of Narcissism* (Warner, 1979)

Malinowski, B: *Sex and Repression in Savage Society* (Routledge, 1960)

Marcuse, Herbert: *One Dimensional Man* (Sphere Books, 1968)
  – *Eros and Civilisation* (Sphere Books, 1969)
Martin, Bernice: *A Sociology of Contemporary Cultural Change* (Blackwell, 1981)
Masters, W H & Johnson, V E: *Human Sexual Response* (Churchill, 1966)
Mead, Margaret: *Coming of Age in Samoa* (Pelican Books, 1960)
Mitchell, J: *Psychoanalysis and Feminisim* (London, 1973)
Parsons, T: *Social Structure and Personality* (The Free Press, 1970)
Piaget, Jean: *The Origin of Intelligence in Children* (International Universities Press, 1952)
  – 'The Stages of the Intellectual Development of the Child' (*Bulletin of the Menniger Clinic 1962*)
Popper, Karl: *Conjectures and Refutations* (Routledge, 1963)
Pribram, K H: *Languages of the Brain* (Prentice Hall, 1971)
Prigogine, I: *From Being to Becoming* (Freeman, NY, 1980)
Reich, Wilhelm: *Character Analysis* (Vision Press, 1951)
  – *The Function of the Orgasm* (Farrar, Strauss & Giroux, 1961)
  – *The Mass Psychology of Fascism* (Souvenir Press, 1972)
  – *The Sexual Revolution* (Vision Press, 1972)
  – *The Cancer Biopathy* (Vision Press, 1973)
Reik, Theodor: *The Unknown Murderer* (Hogarth Press, 1936)
  – *Masochism in Modern Man* (Farrar & Rinehart, 1941)
Ricoeur, Paul: *Freud and Philosophy* (Yale, 1970)
Riesman, D: *The Lonely Crowd* (New Haven, 1950)
Robinson, Paul: *The Sexual Radicals* (Paladin, 1972)
Roheim, G: *Psychoanalysis of Primitive Cultural Types* (New York, 1950)
Roszak, T: *The Making of a Counter Culture* (Faber, 1971)
Sandler, J (ed.): *Dimensions of Psychoanalysis* (Karnac, 1989)
Sandler, J & Freud, Anna: *The Analysis of Defence* (International Universites Press, 1985)

Schopenhauer, Arthur: 'Transcendent Speculation on Apparent Design in the Fate of the Individual' in *Parerga and Paralipomena* (Berlin, 1851)

Schrödinger, E: *What is Life? Mind and Matter* (CUP, 1944)

Segal, Hanna: *Introduction to the Work of Melanie Klein* (Karnac Books, 1973)

Sorokin, P: *Society, Culture and Personality* (NY, 1943)

Spence, D P: *Narrative Truth and Historical Truth* (W W Norton, 1982)

Spezzano, Charles: *Affect in Psychoanalysis* (The Analytic Press, 1993)

Stekel, W: *Sadism and Masochism* (Liveright Publication Company, 1939)

– *Patterns of Psychosexual Infantilism* (Peter Nevill, 1953)

Sterba, R: *Introduction to the Psychoanalytic Theory of the Libido* (N M D Publication Company, 1942)

Stewart, W A: *Psychoanalysis – The First Ten Years* (Allen & Unwin, 1969)

Sullivan, H S: *The Interpersonal Theory of Psychiatry* (Norton, 1953)

Sulloway, F: *Freud: Biologist of the Mind* (Basic Books, 1979)

Wilson, Arnold & Gedo, John E (eds): *Hierarchical Concepts in Psychoanalysis* (Guildford Press, 1993)

Winnicott, D W: *Collected Papers* (Tavistock, 1958)

– *The Maturation Process and the Facilitating Environment* (Hogarth Press, 1960)

– *The Family and Individual Developments* (Basic Books, 1965)

Yankelovich, D & Barrett, W: *Ego and Instinct* (Vintage Books, New York, 1971)

Zilboorg, G: *Sigmund Freud – His Explorations of the Mind* (New York, 1951)

– *Freud's Fundamental Psychiatric Orientation* (NY, 1954)

Index

The Social History of the Unconscious

by George Frankl

is now available in 2 paperback volumes

Vol. 1 Archaeology of the Mind

ISBN 1 871871 16 6 p/b £8.95 232pp

In this book, Frankl applies the techniques of psychoanalysis to recent archaeological findings to trace the psychological development of humanity.

His method enables us to gain a new understanding of how the mind originated, how our earliest ancestors became toolmakers, and how cultures developed. We are shown the conflict between matriarchy and patriarchy, and above all, the nature of patriarchal paranoia, that fatal disease which was and continues to be the source of warfare.

His conclusions are bound to transform some of our fundamental concepts about our social existence.

Vol. 2 Civilisation:
Utopia and Tragedy

ISBN 1 871871 17 4 p/b £8.95 256pp

With this volume we enter history and, in particular, the history of Western civilisation. Through his examination of the unconscious driving forces which produced the great ideas of monotheism, Greek philosophy, democracy and scientific reasoning, Frankl enables us to gain important insights into the conflicts of civilisation and its failures to fulfil its aspirations. By its world-wide influence, the West has assumed an unprecedented responsibility for humanity everywhere, and indeed, for the survival of the planet. But in order to meet those responsibilities, we have to understand the causes of our failures.

The scholarship is prodigious ... today and for the first time I have been properly introduced to my ancestors.
Dr. Peter Randell

One takes it almost for granted that Frankl writes with great intellectual power and lucidity, but it is his generosity and kindness which I find particularly impressive.
Prof. Eva Wolf, Vienna University

For me, this book has joined that group of books which make for compulsive reading – a book that is difficult to put down until it has been read from cover to cover – and one which should be in every doctor's personal library. I cannot wait for the second volume! Dr. Philip Hopkins, Journal of the Balint Society

A learned, carefully argued and densely written book which should be read by anyone interested in the humanities.
Prof. Paul Kline, British Journal of Medical Psychology

The Unknown Self
by George Frankl
ISBN 1 871871 05 5 h/b £16.50
ISBN 1 871871 18 2 p/b £7.95
240pp

This book is based upon Frankl's observations as a psycho-analytic therapist over a period of some thirty-five years. He began his psychoanalytic work in what would nowadays be called the 'classical' mould of psychoanalysis, but extended and deepened Freud's concepts, opening up new dimensions of the psyche which were not accessible to the pioneers. His method of hypnoid analysis makes it possible for patients to remember and to re-live some of the long-forgotten experiences of their lives, thus expanding the boundaries of our understanding of the unconscious mind. *The Unknown Self* traces the psychological development of individuals from early infancy, and shows how a wide range of neurotic and psychotic conflicts originate It combines rigorous scholarship with a deep humanity, which will enable the reader to experience illuminating moments of self-recognition and provide a new understanding of the often baffling behaviour of children.

The Unknown Self *is, quite simply and without unnecessary hyperbole, stupendous! I have never read anything so penetrating and enlightening.*
Dr. Edward Roth

... profound insights, humanity and passion.
Stephen Davy, *Oxford Times*

BIBL. LONDIN. UNIV.